MAHASHAKTI AWAKES

An Autobiography of Spiritual Awakening

Santosh Sachdeva

YogiImpressions®

MAHASHAKTI AWAKES
First published in India in 2018 by
Yogi Impressions LLP
1711, Centre 1, World Trade Centre,
Cuffe Parade, Mumbai 400 005, India.
Website: www.yogiimpressions.com

First Edition, August 2018

Back cover photo: Nikhil Kripalani

ISBN 978-93-82742-95-1

Printed at: SAP Print Solutions Pvt. Ltd., Mumbai

Dedicated to
my loving parents

CONTENTS

Appendixes

MY EARLY DAYS

I was born in 1939 at Sialkot, a flourishing city in what was then known as West Punjab. Ours was a fairly wealthy Punjabi Hindu Brahmin family, who lived in the upscale area known as Greenwood Street. The family continued to live in a rambling old three-storeyed house, although my father had constructed a brand new modern house next to the old house. The new house was quite a landmark in the area, mainly because it was connected to the existing old house by a high bridge that spanned the street. A large private ground fronted the old house, which had a stable for the horse and carriage at one end and a barn for the two cows at the other. Here also was a garage for the station wagon that my father had bought from a British officer, who was leaving for England after serving his tenure. In the centre of the ground were swings for us children and our friends to play.

As a child, I remember going for rides in a *tonga,* which was drawn by a sturdy chestnut-brown horse and driven by our old retainer, Paayi, a *sardar* with a salt-and-pepper beard. If the horse came across a ramshackle hut along the way, he would start neighing and kicking and halt in his tracks, creating quite a panic among us. I often felt petrified and would anxiously wait for him to calm down. Otherwise he was a fairly mild creature, who would allow our younger brother to run under his belly and in and around his legs without kicking up a fuss.

My father—Om Prakash Sharma

My mother—Janki Devi Sharma

Our father was a manufacturer of sporting goods, including cricket bats, hockey sticks, and footballs. His workforce was comprised mainly of Muslim skilled craftsmen, as well as three invaluable retainers—Paayi, Prem, and Babu, who was Prem's younger brother. His clientele were mainly British citizens. Besides supplying his sporting goods to the British soldiers stationed in India, he also exported a large part of his goods to England during the days of the British Raj. The close business ties my father held to these British soldiers led eventually to a more familial link: in fact, the new house my father had built was inaugurated by the chief British officer whom my parents had once invited for high tea in the house's so-called "Drawing Room." That was the only room to have been hastily furnished for the occasion with sofa sets, tea tables, and tapestries imported from England.

The rest of the new house remained unoccupied and unfurnished, with all the imported furniture, chinaware, tapestry, and lighting remaining unpacked in cases in various rooms. Perhaps there was a sense of foreboding of what was soon to come.

My mother sometimes spoke in later years of how I almost had my right foot amputated when I was barely five months old and how I was fortunately saved from spending an entire lifetime as a cripple. My right ankle had developed a boil that had turned septic. Her mother-in-law suggested that the local barber be called in to give it a simple nick and cut to clean it up. My mother recounts that when that day came, every family member, unable to bear the sight of the barber's razor glistening in his hand, left the room. Meanwhile, my mother was left alone to stoically hold me, a screaming infant, in her arms, while the barber made the incision and scraped away at the tissue and bone to remove the infection. He explained that he had to do this to kill the worms, which could be seen wriggling around in the pus. He then applied some disinfectant to the wound. Even after days, the wound continued to ooze and refused to heal.

My mother then took me to the Mayo Hospital in Lahore, where a group of enthusiastic young interns gathered around us. It was wartime then, and there wasn't much room in the hospital. But seeing my mother's plight, one of the interns said that by sheer luck there was a bed available in the crowded hospital, where they recommended that my right foot be amputated without further delay. My mother said that she alone could not take such a major decision without consulting my father. She thanked the intern and made good her escape.

She returned to Sialkot and, as luck would have it, a well-known Bengali surgeon had just arrived in town. I was soon taken to his clinic. He examined the wound and gave my mother the assurance that my ankle was nothing to be alarmed about. Apparently, a splinter of the bone had been inadvertently left inside by the barber, which was what was causing all the trouble. He then very efficiently removed the splinter and put a plaster cast on my foot, leaving a small hole in it to drain out the fluid. I learned to walk and ride a tricycle while still wearing a plaster cast, which ran almost up to the knee of my right leg. The wound soon healed, leaving just a rather ugly scar, one which is still visible to this day on my right ankle.

I was a thin and dark child. The simile my mother sometimes gave me was, "You were as dark as the back of a *tava*." The matter of my foot mercifully, and perhaps providentially, not being amputated proved a huge relief for everyone. It would not only have been painful for them to observe but also a matter of some future concern to have a dark, skinny girl with a physical handicap.

In the wake of Partition in 1947, when the Hindu-Muslim riots erupted, my father's employee Rashid told my father one night that rioters were planning to burn the areas around our house. Heeding Rashid's advice to leave our house, my father sent us to the bungalow of our family physician, Dr. L. C. Dutt, a place situated in the relatively safe zone of the Cantonment. From the bungalow's terrace, we could see spirals of smoke rising from different quarters, which were alarmingly close to the street on which we lived.

One day, our father was strolling on the terrace and gazing at the burning city when he spotted a man in the street pointing a gun toward him. This naturally got my father quite unnerved, and he quickly came down from the terrace to conceal himself from the gunman. Rashid, who sometimes came to visit us in the Cantonment, told our father that he and his people could no longer ensure our safety in the bungalow and advised my father to get his family on a train leaving for Jammu until things settled down. After saying this, Rashid managed to get tickets on a train that was scheduled to leave Sialkot in a few days. Our father meanwhile went back with him to the old house to collect some belongings.

The trip, however, was not to be!

Rashid came to us the evening before the train was set to leave and told my father to cancel the journey, as there was a rumour circulating about that a mob was planning a bloody massacre along the train's route. After much thought and on the advice of the good doctor and his wife, our father decided to move us all to Jammu via a different route to a place where my *Mamaji* lived. Hedo Uberoi, a close friend of my father, very generously offered one of his cars, along with a driver, to bring us to Jammu. Our three servants followed in a tonga as soon as they possibly could, with a few trunks containing some of our belongings.

On the road to Jammu, the car stalled, and the grown-ups had to get out to push it. Fortunately for us, it got going right before a rowdy band of sword-wielding Muslims, who had been hiding in the bushes, came out screaming and began chasing the car.

On reaching Jammu, we stayed for almost a month with our Mamaji. In the past, we had spent some good times visiting him and his family during our holidays. He would take us and our cousins for a swim in what was a fairly large pond. We would take along with us a basketful of small mangoes, tied in a piece of cloth, which we would then dip into the water to keep cool. Once the mangoes had cooled, we would feast on them to our hearts' content. Jammu held good memories for us.

A week later, the news reached us that a convoy of tongas had been massacred. Our father went to the hospital where all the wounded had been taken, but he did not find any of his retainers—Paayi, Prem, or Babu—so he returned quite crestfallen. However, we learned the next day they had somehow managed to escape the attack and had made it safely to Jammu.

Since my father did not want to overstay his welcome at his in-law's place, he decided to take us to Amritsar, where the family's *kul guru* had his *ashram*. So we joined a group of families who had hired a bus to make the trip to Amritsar. Since there were not enough seats to accommodate everyone, the passengers, with the consent of the driver, removed all the seats, packing whatever baggage the families had into the empty spaces. Dhurries were then spread out over trunks and suitcases, so everyone could have a place to sit. Someone's grandfather, in his wisdom and foresight, had filled a bag with roasted gram and peanuts, and during the journey, whenever anyone felt hungry, the old man would give them a fistful to eat.

When the bus reached the banks of the River Ravi, which was about sixty kilometres from Amritsar, everyone was horrified to see that the river was flooded. All the elders had to get out and walk across the river, while the children were ferried across in the bus, which, with its lighter load, was now able to reach the other side of the shore. Once there, everyone unloaded their baggage, and our group joined a convoy of moving humanity. The next river had to be crossed by walking across a two-foot wide bridge without any kind of railing that one could hold onto for support. This was such a fearful experience for some women carrying babies that quite a few of them, in sheer panic and exhaustion, let the screaming babies slip out of their arms and fall into the raging waters.

When a family managed to get any mode of transport—a bullock cart, a tonga, or a jeep—once they forded the river, they would move on. I was around eight years old and have a hazy memory of us sitting in a bullock cart, trying somehow to take cover from the heavy downpour. I also remember our little sister Tuti, who must have then been about six months old, clapping her hands gleefully at the heavy drops of rain splattering over her face. Further along the way, our hearts were warmed to see a row of villagers with pots of chapatis, daal, and water, which they kept warm with wood fires to feed the tired and hungry convoy of refugees. Had it not been for the collective effort of these kind-hearted village folk to serve those of us in distress, many would have probably starved to death from hunger and thirst.

On reaching Amritsar, we all bid our farewells, and each family left to make arrangements to further journey to the towns and villages where their relatives lived. But for us, the kul guru's ashram became our home for some months. While we were lodged inside a room of the ashram, we became acquainted with several other families, who had taken refuge there as well. Space being a constraint, some of them had put up tents on the grounds of the ashram. Everyone had to cook their own food over makeshift fires as the ashram could not feed so many. At night, some good Samaritans from the town would come and hand out blankets to those who needed them for the night. Such scenes were witnessed even on the streets of Amritsar, wherever fleeing families had managed to pitch tents in the parks or wherever they huddled in some corner of the town's footpaths. I also recall that one of our father's relatives was seen selling roasted gram and peanuts in town to those who had the money to buy them.

I don't quite remember how long we stayed at the ashram; it may have been a month or so. One day, our father told my mother that he had somehow managed to charter a Dakota plane to fly us to Delhi. On arriving in the capital, we checked into a rather run down hotel, ironically named Regal Hotel, in what is today known as Paharganj. From the balcony of our room, we could look down on cars, buses, and pedestrians, negotiating their way along the busy street.

One afternoon, as he was standing on the balcony of the hotel, my father spotted a cousin of his in the street below. He shouted out, "Yograj, Yograj!" and waved his white hanky to attract his cousin's attention. Yograj stopped in his tracks and looked around and up to see who was calling out his name. After seeing my father in his trademark white *salwar-kurta* waving at him, he came up to the hotel. The chance meeting led to our moving out of the hotel and into the railway quarters at Subzi Mandi, where Yograj lived with his wife, Rakho, and sister, Bimla. Although their quarters comprised just two rooms and a kitchen, there was a fairly spacious garden enclosed within it, where we could play around. I do recall there were one or two banana plants growing in it, apart from some shrubs and flowers. So there we were, eight members of our family and three of theirs, cramped up in just two small rooms. But they were happy to have us, and not once did they make us feel that we were overstaying our welcome.

During this time, Rashid came from Sialkot to visit us in Delhi and brought a few of our belongings with him. He suggested that my father go back with him to Pakistan, probably because he could quite easily pass off as a Muslim. He assured him he would do all that he could to help my father bring some of the family's wealth back that had been left behind. Our father took him up on the offer and going straight to his bank in Sialkot, withdrew all his jewelry, along with whatever savings he could safely bring back with him. But he left the keys of both houses with Rashid.

It was during this time—January 30, 1948, to be precise—that Mahatma Gandhi was shot while coming out of his evening prayers at Birla Mandir in Delhi. The whole country moaned and wept. Songs came out almost overnight on the life of Gandhi, but the one that became probably most popular was one sung by Mohammed Rafi, "Suno Suno ai Duniyawalo, Bapu ki yeh Amar Kahani." My father, who was quite patriotically inclined, immediately went out and bought the double-record set and kept replaying it on the gramophone over and over again until we would beg him to stop! His obsession with this record, along with those of K. L. Saigal (which he had brought back from his trip to Pakistan), lasted quite a few years.

After spending about six months with our relatives in Delhi, it must have dawned on Papaji that we were overstaying the hospitality offered to us. One of my father's business managers, called Mulkhraj, who had settled in Jullunder after the Partition, came to see us, and he advised my father to move to Jullunder and start his sporting business afresh. To this day, I still don't know what must have influenced our father's response to this proposition. Instead he asked Mulkhraj to go to a nearby hill station, called Mussoorie, to look for a place where he could take his family for the summer. Mulkhraj scouted around the hill station and came back to inform him that he had booked a big bungalow, called Dil Bahar (which means "celebrative heart" in Hindi), in Happy Valley.

So, packing our meagre belongings, we drove up to Mussoorie. It was raining heavily when we reached the outskirts of the hill station, from where we had to take a ride in hand-drawn rickshaws pulled by five natives, to reach Dil Bahar, which would become our home for the next twenty years or so.

Arriving at Dil Bahar, we were taken straight up to the bedrooms and put into the beds. Our mother covered us with quilts, warmed by hot water bottles that had been thoughtfully placed out on a table by the *chowkidar* of the bungalow. The next morning, we woke up feeling excited to be in such a new and interesting place. We went about the house, exploring it and going from room to room. We discovered shortly thereafter, the house contained twelve rooms and eight bathrooms. Much to our delight, there were two playgrounds—a large one at the back of the house and another fairly spacious one that ran along its side and frontage. *Bebeji*, our paternal grandmother, promptly converted one of the smaller rooms into a temple. She covered one wall completely with holy pictures and installed a small wooden temple as a sanctum to hold the statues of the principal gods and goddesses, a *Shiva lingam*, and an *aasan*. This small room could also be accessed by a wooden staircase that went up to it from the ground at the back of the house. After her morning and evening *puja*, she would perform *aarti* and then take the first offering of food, cooked in the kitchen, up to the gods before serving it to the family.

Our father meanwhile settled into a life of early retirement while he was just in his mid-thirties. Although people were initially rather cool to his presence and kept aloof, suspecting that he was a Muslim man who had eloped with the daughter of a Hindu Brahmin family, their speculations ended when they

Our father always wore the traditional dress of Pakistani men, a white salwar-kurta with an *achkan*

discovered he was really a Hindu who had adopted the mode of dress favoured by men in Pakistan. Eventually, he went on to become a prominent and popular figure in Mussoorie's rather uppity, affluent, sophisticated society.

Once we got accustomed to the new environment, our mother, who was concerned that we were missing out on schooling, enrolled us into an English-medium school, the Convent of Jesus and Mary, which was about a twenty-minute walk from our home. Before leaving for school, we would quickly go to the temple, get down on our knees, and touch our heads to the ground before the gods in their sanctum. Bebeji would then pour a spoonful of *charanamrit* into our cupped palms, which we would drink. We would then rush out of the temple, put our shoes back on, and head off for school. We would reach school at nine o'clock in the morning and come home by four in the afternoon.

The compound at the back was generally referred to as the "kirket" ground because it was once used by the Nawab who owned Dil Bahar and played cricket with his lackeys when he lived there. Our mother now turned it into a beautiful playground for us, with flower beds running along its four sides. On the sloping terraced fields, which led from the road above the house, there were apple and apricot trees, and a variety of vegetables growing abundantly. On the lower field, a sturdy branch of a beautiful apricot tree held a swing with a wooden plank as its seat. The walls on three sides of the house were covered with creeper vines of Dutch roses and passion flowers. In the flowerbeds running at the base of the walls grew clutches of nasturtiums and pansies; marigolds and dahlias dominated the tiny flowers growing beneath them. Our mother had a "green thumb," as they say, and Dil Bahar was a riot of gardening colour for the better part of the year.

In addition to an extensive garden, my mother had several pets, including lovebirds, pigeons, goats, hens, and even a baby deer. There were always four to five dogs of different breeds wandering around, whom we used to protect the house from leopards, which would come down from the snowy peaks during the severe winter months. The house evolved into a kind of fairyland for us, changing its outward appearance as the seasons changed from spring to summer, from monsoon to autumn, and from autumn to the onset of snow in winter. Life took on a different rhythm from what it had been in Sialkot.

Being a fairly prominent member of Mussoorie society, our family was at the forefront of greeting Indian and foreign dignitaries, who visited our hill station and who were usually feted at one or the other of its two leading hotels, The Savoy and Hakmans. Thus, it was that when Jawaharlal Nehru visited Mussoorie, he was felicitated at Hakmans.

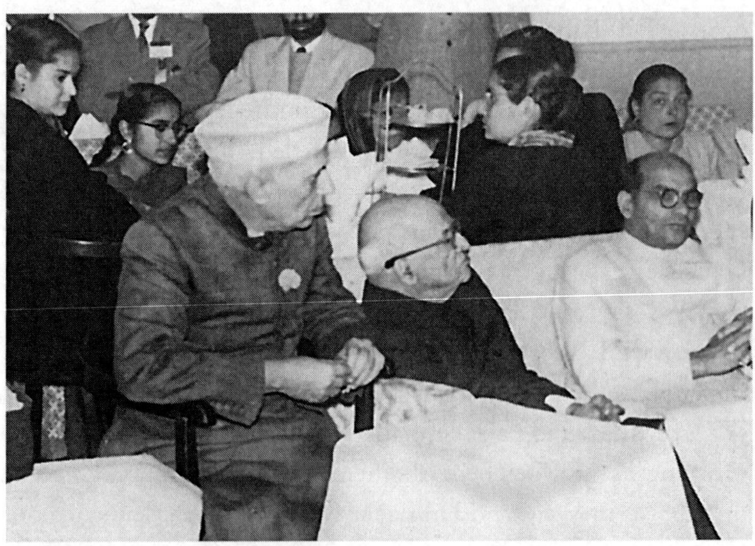

My family (seated behind) at a reception to welcome Jawaharlal Nehru at Hakmans Hotel

My mother (in white *sari* at left) at the function to welcome His Holiness the Dalai Lama at Mussoorie

My father had an affinity for men and women in white or saffron robes. *Sadhus* travelling to and from the Himalayas were a familiar sight at our bungalow, where they would rest awhile or stay for a few days, and it was this that distinguished our bungalow from many others in town.

I first had the privilege of paying homage to His Holiness the Dalai Lama when he left Tibet in 1959 to seek asylum in India. The government had accommodated him at Birla House in Happy Valley, while the refugees who had escaped with him were put up in nearby houses. Soon after, leading citizens of Mussoorie arranged a reception to welcome and honour His Holiness at The Savoy Hotel, an event to which our whole family was invited.

Down the years, my family also had a few other encounters with various dignitaries. The Mussoorie ladies' society, which did social work to benefit the poorer sections of people in the nearby villages, coaxed my mother one year into joining their ranks. For the inauguration of one of the society's projects at Bhatta Falls, my mother, along with some of the ladies in the society, escorted Indira Gandhi around the village where the project was underway. Another memorable moment in my family's history came when His Highness Haile Selassie, the Ethiopian emperor, graced our town. The last direct descendant from the line of the biblical King Solomon, he was felicitated at a lavish banquet in his honour at The Savoy.

Altruistic by nature, my parents held an open house for most part of the year. Our mother took care of everyone's needs, not only looking after the sadhus, sages, and their disciples who arrived at the bungalow but also after the visiting relatives and our school friends who would occasionally drop by. She taught me the value of believing that our focus in life should be only

Indira Gandhi being accompanied by my mother (centre) to Bhatta Falls

on the positive aspects of our experience; the negative aspects, she told me, should be ignored. My father was an active member of CARE Australia, a global humanitarian organisation that helps the poor and needy. He was the organisations's Indian representative for several years, and in this capacity, he worked on distributing milk powder, syrup, and cheese to the poor from the villages in and around Mussoorie.

An impressionable young schoolgirl, I came under the influence of Christianity at Waverley—Convent of Jesus and Mary. The school had a fairly sizeable chapel on the premises, with marble bowls on either side of its entrance, into which we would occasionally dip our fingers and make the sign of the cross before entering our classes. The annual concert in December was marked by piano recitals, singing, and short plays revolving around Christmas themes. When I was in the ninth standard, the annual concert was based on Jesus Christ and Mary Magdalene.

My father (centre) with my mother next to him, distributing milk powder to the villagers

Because I was the tallest among the girls in my class, I was selected to play the role of Jesus with my long hair curled up in ringlets that fell to my shoulders. Even at that young age, the role filled me with awe, and I felt a physical change in my posture and carriage.

THE FAMILY GURU: SWAMI MOHAN GIRI

Our kul guru Swami Mohangiriji 108

My grandparents, father, and mother revered their kul guru, whose name was *Swami* Mohangiri. Generally, we would address him respectfully as Swamiji. Along with his entourage consisting of three or four young sadhus, he would spend a month or so every year with us, living in a separate wing of the bungalow specially allotted to visiting holy men. My two sisters, one brother, and I grew up in an atmosphere graced by his presence. We were quite used to coming back from school to find the house and garden full of saffron-clad *sannyasis.* Some of them became my friends, and I discovered I could talk to them quite freely and even confide with them about my problems. While Swamiji was staying with us, the daily routine would begin with us going to him to offer our *pranaams* and receive his blessings before going to school. In the evening, we would spend some time with him and attend the aarti and prayers. The atmosphere in the bungalow would often resonate with the rhythmic sound of *mantras* chanted by him and the young sadhus.

I remember Swamiji as a rather gentle and genial person, in whose presence I felt very comfortable. A smile always played around on his rather roundish face. There were no barriers between us, and it was possible to communicate with him on any subject. One had the freedom of making mistakes, learning from them, and going back to him knowing that he would always understand.

The first couple of years of growing up in Mussoorie breezed by. The only unpleasant part of it was having to go to school early in the morning. But as time progressed, I felt more comfortable in the atmosphere of the Convent of Jesus and Mary, with its beautiful chapel. The school's spacious main ground was remarkable for its big merry-go-round. The other playgrounds nearby were shaded by tall *deodar* trees.

When I was thirteen or fourteen years old, my grandmother asked me one morning to have my bath and come straight to Swamiji's room. Upon entering I saw special lamps ready to be lit, a basket of flowers, and other preparations for a puja. I was then made to go through the traditional ceremony of initiation.

Swamiji gave me a short *Shiva mantra*, and I was told to chant it daily, as often as I wanted. At no stage was I asked whether I wanted to be initiated. My mother had earlier taught us the *Gayatri mantra*, which she would have us recite daily. In addition to that, I now had my own special mantra. It was several years later that my mother told me that the *mantra diksha*, or initiation, had been given in keeping with the express wishes of Swamiji. I was the only one of her children to have been singled out—for reasons best known to Swamiji.

After completing my schooling in Mussoorie, I left home at age sixteen to join Miranda House, a college for women at Delhi University. I returned home after graduation to teach for a couple of years at my alma mater. As a young woman, I now started attracting a string of admirers, young men who were training for the Indian Administrative or Foreign Service cadre at the National Academy of Administration, which had recently shifted from Delhi to Mussoorie.

Several proposals of marriage began pouring in, but somehow the young men appeared rather immature to me. Although they mostly wore their hearts on their sleeves, I had to disappoint them.

A couple of them, now married and well settled into senior positions, continue to stay in touch. We meet once every few years when they are in town over nostalgic cups of tea to compare notes on where our lives have led us.

Mantra Power

I remember one particular summer during which I was rather distressed. I had fallen for a young man who was already in love with someone else. As a matter of fact, he had tailed me like Mary's little lamb throughout his year's stay at the academy in Mussoorie. However his girlfriend, who lived somewhere in the plains, did not appreciate my interests in him and threatened to take extreme measures to secure her relationship with him. At the time, I felt caught up in this triangle, which was not really of my own making.

I went through a period of confusion and confrontations, feeling betrayed and also angry because of threats and emotional blackmail. I did not quite know what to do, and so I thought about talking it over with Swamiji. He was sympathetic and gave me a mantra. He asked me to get up early in the morning, wear white clothes, collect white flowers, and sit in the puja room to recite the mantra. I was told to complete a *mala* of 108 beads every morning, stopping at once if I felt uncomfortable, as there was immense power in the mantras.

During this time, one of his young disciples, whom we called Chhota Mahatma, gave me his cherished picture of Shiva and Parvati. In my usual hurry to get on with things, I would get up early, have a bath, put on a sari, and then rush to collect white flowers from our garden in the cricket ground. After this, I would go up the wooden steps leading to my grandmother's small puja room. I would sit on the aasan, light the lamp and incense, and follow Swamiji's strict instructions. I was so comfortable with the mantra that I began to complete two, three, and occasionally more repetitions of the mala at a time.

One day, while I was doing extra repetitions of the mala, I saw a movement in the picture of Shiva and Parvati that was before me. Parvati's face, which had been in her normal pose of gazing at Shiva, turned toward me with eyes full of anger. I thought I was hallucinating. Quite unnerved, I closed my eyes and continued moving the beads of the mala. After some time, I ventured to open an eye and look at the picture again. Parvati was still looking at me with angry eyes. Panicked, I dropped the mala and ran to Swamiji, who was staying in the room opposite the temple. With quaking voice and a fear-ridden face, I told him of what had just occurred. He asked me to stop the mantra at once, and reciting a mantra, he sprinkled a few drops of water on me from his *kamandalu*.

The powerful, energised picture of Shiva and Parvati gifted to me by Chhota Mahatma

This calmed me down, and at that moment, I was permanently cured of my infatuation with the young man.

This incident served to instill a deep respect within me for the power of mantras.

On a small hill, across the valley from Dil Bahar, stood the Katesar Castle, a replica of England's Windsor Castle. At some distance from the castle, the Raja of Katesar had built a small marble temple, dedicated to Radha Krishna. His three children were also studying at the same school with us, which meant that we started visiting each other's homes on our respective birthdays and on other festive occasions, especially on Janmashtami. Every time we went over, we also visited this temple for *darshan* of Radha and Krishna. I would often visualise myself dressed in a white sari, carrying a basket of flowers and walking across the valley to the temple atop the hill. That visualisation alone would make me feel euphoric.

The Radha Krishna temple at Katesar Castle

SAGE FROM THE SOUTH

Sometime in 1950, my father heard about a certain sage from South India who was visiting Mussoorie. He decided to invite the old man to our home, as, you may recall, we were quite used to sadhus staying a few days with us before they went higher up into the Himalayas. When the sage arrived, we saw the man, who appeared to be at least eighty years old, was very frail and that he seemed to be perpetually in a trance-like state. He was accompanied by some junior sadhus, two casually dressed American men, and a fairly young woman. The three foreigners appeared to be hippies, who were constantly in a drug-induced haze.

Clad only in a loincloth, the thin-as-a-reed old sage attracted quite a large crowd. People from around who became his devotees would bring *nimbu* as an offering to him, which he would bless and return to them. Many believed that this would somehow help to get their wishes fulfilled. People would start congregating around in the early evening and sit in the cricket ground behind the house. Among his sadhus was a dark, young novitiate by the name of Sambandham, an enthusiastic seeker on the spiritual path. He would narrate his experiences with the aged swami and his divinity, his fondness for him, and the blessings he felt when the swami's grace engulfed him. Sambandham had a certain calm and presence about him that created a strong impression and left a vivid memory on my mind. After staying with us for a week, the band of sadhus left for Rishikesh. I don't know what must have transpired because we later heard that Sambandham had dropped out of the group at Rishikesh and gone back to mainstream life.

The constant flow of sadhus and their entourages—housing them, cooking for them, and feeding them—must have been quite a strain on my mother. As children, we were quite obedient. I don't remember any of us protesting whenever we would be asked to move out of our rooms to accommodate the sadhus. Things were not always so pleasant, though. In their drugged state, the hippies, who were put up in a room next to the prayer room, would not know in which direction to go to the toilet at night and would sometimes end up urinating in a corner of the room.

The massive *yagna,* which this sadhu from the south organised at our house and which our father thought was certain to halt the decline in his fortunes, did not bear the desired results. This event, more than anything else, disheartened him and led to his eventual disenchantment with the sadhus and sages. However, I feel my mother was quite relieved at having to perform less hospitality.

BENGALI MAHATMA

When I would come home to Mussoorie from college during the term holidays, I would often see a young sadhu with shoulder-length, jet-black locks sitting on the porch with my parents. He would occasionally drop by while on his barefoot walk from his quarters in Kulri to Happy Valley. Before going back, he would take a break at Dil Bahar, chat with us, and have a glass of milk and some fruits my mother would serve. He was often dressed in a white djellaba-like garment.

Our grandmother had passed on in the winter of 1962. In the same year, our father decided to leave the sprawling mansion of Dil Bahar and move into a smaller house in the central part of the town. This was probably because he found the long walk from Dil Bahar to the main part of the hill station an arduous one. Another reason was that my elder sister had left Mussoorie for further studies in Bombay and I was in Delhi. He found a small cottage named Shamrock Lodge, which was below the road that led from Kincraig, the main bus terminus on the road to Mussoorie, to Library Bazaar, the hub of Mussoorie from 1948 onwards.

Once we moved into Shamrock Lodge, we would often meet the young sadhu (we never got to know his actual name because he didn't speak at all) on our regular evening walks. By this time he had retreated into complete *maun vrat*, a vow of silence, and one could only communicate with him through a smile, a nod, or a gesture. One cannot explain why we felt a close and familiar bond with him. Perhaps it was his smile and expression that was always serene, or perhaps it was a kind of joy in his stride. He radiated a feeling of belonging and unconditional love.

Whenever we would see him coming, we would stop and wish him well. He would also stop. We would talk, and he would listen. Then, raising both his hands in blessing, he would move on without saying anything. Yet one was left with the feeling that we had actually exchanged some words with him.

GOOD AND NOT-SO-GOOD SPIRITS

There is a certain sense of companionship, joy, and freedom growing up in a small hill station where everyone knows everyone. It was in this spirit of concern and caring that the youth of Mussoorie came together in 1962 to organise a variety entertainment show to raise money for the Defence of India Fund during the India-China War of that same year. Hakmans Hotel generously gave us the use of their hall and stage for both the rehearsals and the final show. The three-day event was fully managed and put together by a band of youth comprised of college-going students and sons of local tradesmen, including those of local electricians, gardeners, chowkidars, and municipal clerks. These youth handled the entire event—everything from production, direction, acting, and costume design to lights, music, and stage backdrops. The only adults involved in the event included a well-known author and a classical dance teacher.

A highlight of the show was a short play on the life of Gautama Buddha. After much debating about which one of the boys would be suitable for the role of Buddha—a process that failed to choose any one of the males auditioning—it was decided that I should play the Buddha, as I was the tallest of the girls. While enacting that role, I imbibed without realising it a sense of humility and sensitivity to the human condition, as well as a gentleness of spirit. In retrospect, I am quite sure that playing that part somehow

Playing the part of Siddhartha, I am bidding farewell to my wife and newborn son before leaving the palace

The final scene: As Gautam Buddha, I visit my wife after attaining 'Nirvana'

enhanced my sense of *vairagya,* or non-attachment to earthly things.

As youngsters, we would sometimes go to a cemetery in the evening and tell ghost stories. The naughtier boys would add to the spooky atmosphere by making weird sounds at the scariest points in the stories. On one such evening, a troublesome spirit latched on to me while coming home from the cemetery. From then on, it would shake me by the shoulder every night at about two in the morning and tell me to get up. Then, it would say, "I have something to tell you."

Scared out of my wits, I would wake up with a start and switch on the lights to see who it was, but I could not feel any presence around me. This went on for a few days. At first, I did not want to tell my parents, as it seemed we already had one spirit in the house. My mother and I would often feel its presence—sometimes even during the afternoon—moving around the house from one room to the other. Finally, I decided to tell my mother about our visit to the cemetery and about the spirit that had been troubling me for the past few nights. She tried different *totkas,* or rituals, to drive it away, all of which were to no avail. Our neighbour suggested that I sleep with a knife under my pillow. Another said that I should put water in a bowl and keep it beside my bed. But nothing worked.

It so happened that a young sadhu came visiting one day, and my father, in his usual affable way, asked him to rest the night at our cottage. My mother suggested that he could leave for the Himalayas after having breakfast the next morning. Since the house did not have a spare guest room, I offered my small room to him for the night. There was a selfish motive in my offer. My brother and I wanted to see if the spirit would disturb him while he slept.

Next morning, we were keenly watching the sadhu's face to see if it appeared disturbed. But he looked calm and peaceful. I couldn't refrain from asking whether he had felt any spirit trying to wake him during the night. He told us that he had not felt any such thing. He had probably evicted the spirit with his holy presence as I was never disturbed by it again.

SATHYA SAI BABA AND HIS PRASAD

Toward the end of 1965, an article appeared in *The Illustrated Weekly of India* featuring a full-length photograph of a young holy man in a long saffron robe with a halo of curly, black hair. Sometime before the magazine carried this article, I remember there had been rumours that a young sadhu matching the same description had come to Mussoorie, whom we thought might be the same one mentioned in the article. Upon hearing this rumour, my father had immediately set out to find him, but unfortunately, the young man had already left our town.

In the early hours of one morning, I had a strange dream. I saw a head of similar curly hair, positioned from the neck upward, mounted on a wall and turning from left to right. It reminded me of the antelope and leopard heads mounted as hunting trophies on the walls of some palaces in Mussoorie. After a few moments, the head on the wall disappeared, and in its place, I saw a figure reclining in the pose similar to that of Lord Vishnu. The figure was that of the young man with the same curly, black hair. In the dream, I saw myself, along with some other people, sitting beside his reclining figure.

As the dream progressed, the young swami gave me *prasad*, a food offering, of two *pedas*. My hands reached out to take the pedas, and I then put them under my pillow. The entire dream was so real that I woke up with a start. My hand searched under the pillow for the pedas, but to my surprise, there was nothing there.

I went looking for the magazine article soon after, and going quickly through its pages, I found the picture of the young swami. I was pleasantly surprised to see it was the same figure I had seen in the dream. I also read that his name was Sathya Sai Baba.

The blessing, given as two pedas in the dream, manifested itself in the next four months.

In January 1966, my sister Raj, who was then engaged to her colleague in Air India, asked my father to send me to Bombay to meet a prospective groom. Although Bombay seemed a long way from home, I somehow mustered up the courage to travel alone by train. My father came with me up to Delhi and put me on the Rajdhani Express. On reaching Bombay, I was received at the station by my sister and would-be brother-in-law.

The meeting with the proposed match, whose name was Ajeet, had been arranged that evening over an informal dinner. After that, Ajeet and I met a couple of times, and somehow things worked out between us. For me it was an easy decision. The man I met and came to know matched the image I had in my mind of what I always wanted—someone with a charismatic personality. We got engaged in February and were married in April 1966. In a couple of months, I was carrying my first child. Sathya Sai Baba once again came in my dream and placed a baby in my outstretched arms. Months later, the baby girl born to me was given the name of Shibani.

When I was expecting my second child, I heard that Sathya Sai Baba had come to an ashram in Andheri, a suburb of Bombay. I went with my mother to have his darshan. We joined a row of people sitting on the ground. As I sat there, I kept asking myself: would Baba, since I was with child, give me two packets of *vibhuti* or only one? As he passed by us, I was completely surprised when he dropped two packets into my lap! My relationship with Sathya Sai Baba has been either through dreams or by darshan at a public gathering. On one occasion, my daughter Shibani, my friend Meena and I went to Puttaparthi and spent three days at Sathya Sai Baba's ashram. Sitting daily in the darshan hall, there was always a feeling of joy and completeness. It was enough to be in his energy field.

My children were born within a few years of each other, and all three of them have come as the most precious of gifts. After their birth, I inculcated the habit in myself of lighting a lamp, sitting down in the front of the altar in my bedroom every morning, and doing *japa* with my mala. I was clearly aware that if they would see me sitting daily at puja, they would sooner or later automatically follow my example in some way or another.

By the time they entered their late twenties, each one of my children had found a path of spirituality best suited to their individual temperaments. Nikki and Gautam gravitated toward the path of *Jnana Yoga,* the path of knowledge, while Shibani chose the *Bhakti*, or devotional, path. Individually, they were led to a spiritual master who met and fulfilled their requirements for spiritual unfoldment.

Shibani was introduced to the Art of Living by friends. She became a devoted follower of Sri Sri Ravi Shankar. Gautam discovered Ramesh Balsekar, who was a disciple of Sri Nisargadatta Maharaj, and had *satsang* at his home in South Mumbai. Nikki, during her years in Hong Kong, came in contact with Master Charles Cannon, a disciple of Swami Muktananda of Ganeshpuri. She later met Eckhart Tolle, author of the best-selling book *The Power of Now*, and is now an ardent follower of his teaching. As they journey on the path of spiritual progress, the three of them have also managed to continue with their full-time professional careers.

MEENA KAPUR: A FRIEND FOR ALL SEASONS

Meena came from a spiritual background. Her aunt was the spiritual head of an ashram in Haridwar, where Meena spent many holidays growing up in the company of sadhus and *sannyasins*. She gravitated toward the bhakti form of spirituality, particularly in her devotion to the Goddess Durga. She has attained devotional fulfillment that expresses itself in her unconditional love for all creation. Meena and I studied in the same college in Delhi. When I lived in the hostel, I would sometimes spend the weekends at her home. Over time, we developed a bond of mutual love and respect for each other, in which we would share mental and emotional issues that usually crop up as one moves through life.

Meena moved to Bombay to pursue her interest in psychology and went in for training to qualify as a psychoanalyst. By this time, I had three young children with very little age difference between them. Meena was a lighthearted and cheerful person—bubbly, spirited, and always happy. She would walk into our house whistling and smiling. I would see my children's faces light up with smiles, and they would feel uplifted in her presence. They adored her and loved it when my husband and I had to go out of Mumbai for a week or two and Meena would move in to babysit. Her presence, coupled with her background in psychology, played an important role during their formative years, both in their adolescence and on into their young adulthood.

Meena's coming to live in Mumbai was a big support to me, especially as I had married into a large family and entered into a phase of playing different roles of wife, mother, *masi, chachi, bhabhi*, and so on. She was a great sounding board who helped me stay balanced and equanimous through thick and thin. I will always treasure our togetherness and soul bond.

Meena loved visiting temples, so we would often visit several temples together. For instance, we took a trip to Shirdi every six months. On one such trip, we undertook a pilgrimage to Solapur, Kolhapur, and Pandharpur, visiting the Mahalakshmi, Ma Tulja Bhavani, and Shiva temples, as well as the shrine of Swami Samarth at Akkalkot.

Meena is very passionate about visiting temples. Even if it is only a small temple by the roadside dedicated to Hanuman, Ganpati, Shiva, Krishna, or Devi, she seems to be magnetically drawn to them. The way I see it is that, with her *sadhana* the way it is and given the kind of person she is, her energy vibration responds to the divine energy surrounding the temples, whether

Meena (left) and I during our college days

Meena and I on a trip to the Ganesha temple at Ganpatipule in 2014

on the roadside or in a large and magnificent temple complex. It is simply a happening. Initially, I would get frustrated when we would suddenly have to stop in the middle of nowhere or in crowded areas because Meena would spot a tiny temple in some corner. But with time, I learnt to accept it, and now I understand why this happens. This irresistible urge is not in her control; her energy vibration is finely tuned to the divine energy.

A CHAPTER CLOSES

In the year 1982, when my children had just about entered their teens, my husband, Ajeet, fell sick with acute abdominal discomfort. After doing the rounds of various doctors and specialists, it was found that he had cancer of the sigmoid colon. He bore his illness with commendable acceptance and patience and by putting on a brave front for his children, friends, and staff. Both our families were a big support, while Meena and I did the rounds of different temples praying for his well-being. We performed a four-hour Devi yagna at the Gamdevi Durga temple, at the end of which we were given prasad of a coconut and flowers. Coming home with the thought of giving this prasad to Ajeet, I asked the cook to break the coconut. He called me to the kitchen and looked at me in a perplexed manner. I saw him holding two empty halves of the coconut shell, and we both looked blankly at each other as we saw that there was no white pulp inside the shells. This was not a good omen. Although I was dismayed, I maintained my composure and calmly asked him not to mention this to anyone and to go immerse the empty shells in the sea.

The very next morning, I went to see Meena and shared my fears that resulted from seeing the coconut shell. She asked me to pray to Ma Durga. Sitting in front of her Durga altar, I asked for a sign. A vision of Ajeet surfaced in my mind, as white as the inside of a coconut. This somehow gave me the assurance that he would pull through.

Ajeet had a good two years after his rounds of chemotherapy. He started going back to the office and managed to put some of his business affairs in order. He even took the family on a holiday to Kashmir. However, once back, his stomach started giving him trouble again, and thus began another round of tests by doctors, who kept assuring us the trouble was only due to adhesions and nothing serious. At one consultation, the doctor suggested we get an X-ray done. After seeing the report, he asked me to admit Ajeet immediately, and he informed me that he would perform surgery the very next day. We were in shock, and I said this was all too sudden; I would need to talk to my family.

My husband, Ajeet, and I on holiday in Pahalgam, Kashmir in 1980

During this time, some strange incidents occurred. Bats had begun hanging on the trees outside our building, and I could see some from our bedroom window. Once, in the middle of the night, I got up to drink water when I heard and saw what seemed to be a fairly big bird fly out of the window. I thought it was a crow but wondered if it could have been a bat. On another occasion, the bedsheet I had kept in the balcony caught fire and burned up in flames. Perhaps it had been caused by someone who had thrown a cigarette from above. I ran to get the tongs from the kitchen, snatched the burning sheet, and threw it out of the balcony into the compound below.

I now regarded these unusual incidents as ominous signs of what was to come.

Ajeet was admitted back into the Breach Candy Hospital, where his abdomen was opened and closed without any surgery being performed. The oncologist and the surgeon came out quietly shaking their heads. Around this time, Jammu Maharaj, a *devi upasak* of repute, had come to visit someone nearby at Carmichael Road. Meena and I went across to request him to come and bless Ajeet. He came willingly with us, stood at the foot of Ajeet's bed, and scanned him with his eyes. Waving a hand in the air, he drew something from it. Opening his palm, he gave me a *chiku* as prasad and told me to get Ajeet to lick it a bit.

I went to leave Jammu Maharaj to the car. While we were walking, he told me that if Ajeet survived till his birthday on November 11, then he would have some years more to live. In the event that did not happen, he said he would not live past September 26. Ajeet passed away on September 26, 1984.

At the time of his passing, Ajeet was at the peak of his career. The advertising agency that he had set up and built after years of hard work had just begun to flourish.

A sketched portrait done as a tribute to my husband, Ajeet Sachdeva

ANOTHER CHAPTER OPENS

After the *uthala* ceremony, on the fourth day after Ajeet's passing, a few of Ajeet's friends accompanied me to the office and asked me to sit on Ajeet's chair in his cabin. Spontaneously, I asked, "Would you all like a cup of coffee?" There was a moment of silence. We must have sat for about half an hour, and they emphasised that I would need to come every day and occupy that chair. The next morning after my bath, I sat down for my japa and spoke to Lord Shiva, telling Him that one chapter had closed and another

At the office desk

had now opened. I had been a housewife and had no idea how to run a business; it was all so new to me. I said to Him, "I know nothing about it. I will do my bit by going and sitting in the chair. The rest, You will have to take care of."

That was exactly what happened.

The next day I reached office and went straight into the cabin. Ajeet's photo was placed on the wall behind my chair. I spoke a few words to him and then asked the staff to come in. I addressed them by saying, "I don't know all of you, but by and by, I will get to know each one of you by name. I don't know anything about advertising, but I am sure with your support, it will all work out." From that day onward, I started attending the office on a daily basis.

One immediate fallout of Ajeet's demise was that the bank froze our account. This experience was a shock to me as it was my first attempt at venturing out of a sheltered life into a business environment, where I was soon to learn that things are quite cut-and-dried and devoid of any feelings. The bank manager at our bank was unresponsive to my appeal to release the funds and refused to budge. I went to other banks with the problem but met with no response. As a last resort, I went to meet Ajeet's good friend Prem Khanna. He willingly came with me to the bank and said he would stand as guarantor. This was a big relief for us as a family.

I remember Ajeet's friends came home one evening and wanted to know whether I knew how to write a cheque. They educated me on that and other routine accounting and operational procedures.

Soon my new role as head of the agency was becoming more defined. I learned to look at the finances and almost beg our clients for the money that was rightfully due to us. This problem with clients defaulting had arisen because the agency had extended a line of credit, as was standard agency practice, to clients who would invariably delay on outstanding payments. And some of them did not pay us at all, leading to a decline in the agency's fortunes. On the other hand, suppliers who did not visit our office for the first one or two years since Ajeet's passing soon began asking to meet me for their long overdue amounts.

One day, the receptionist buzzed me on the intercom and said that a billboard contractor wanted to meet me. He came and sat down opposite me. He was well built, and his stance suggested that he had other ways of collecting his dues. I offered him a cup of coffee and asked about the purpose of his visit. He appeared to ease up and relax, perceiving that I was not a dragon sitting opposite him but a harmless housewife who probably knew nothing about business. He quietly told me the amount that was overdue to him. Since he was a Punjabi, I spoke to him in Punjabi and explained my predicament. I told him that as soon as we collected the amount from our client, we would clear his dues. I don't think he ever asked for his money after that.

My brother, Shiv, was a big support at this time, along with the rest of the team. None of us were business oriented. We didn't know much about things like statutory compliances, company laws, etc. We were all learning on the job. While the staff ran the show in terms of meeting clients, developing advertising campaigns, and dealing with suppliers, I would meet with bank managers or whoever else I was required to visit when any financial matters or crises arose. A typical case of such a crisis was when publications would threaten to block our clients' ads by placing an embargo on the agency due to nonpayment of dues by one of our defaulting clients. It was a tough scenario. Whether or not our clients cleared our dues, we were liable to pay the newspapers on time.

GROWING IN CONFIDENCE

It was during the stressful period in 1983 that a charming lady by the name of Vilas Lokhandwala, then the incoming president of the Lioness Club of Churchgate, came to see me. Lioness Clubs are now part of Lions Clubs International. She talked me into becoming a member of the club, as it was in my locality and actively involved in civic, social, and cultural projects for the community.

From then on, Vilas took it upon herself to see that I attended all the meetings and gatherings. It was in 1984 that she coaxed me

Addressing a meeting as secretary of the Lioness Club, Churchgate

into becoming the secretary of the club. Vilas played a big role in getting me out of the house through various activities of the club. I remember that on the thirteenth day after Ajeet's passing, the Lioness Club's meeting happened to be at The Cricket Club of India, which is just across from our home. Vilas came over and would not leave unless I accompanied her. Not only that, she also saw to it that I got up and gave a vote of thanks at the end.

Though I was rather upset by her insistence, it eventually did work in my favour to ensure that I didn't become socially shy and cocooned. I had become an integral part of this warm, friendly group of ladies, whose support helped me in the transition from being a homemaker to a fairly successful business woman with an active social life. Slowly but steadily, I became a more confident person who developed her own distinctive individuality.

One of the high points of my tenure at the club was the honouring of Padma Shri Murlidhar Devidas Amte. Popularly

Receiving an award for the best secretary at the Lioness Club, Churchgate

known as Baba Amte, he was an Indian social activist well known for his tireless work in the rehabilitation and empowerment of poor people afflicted with and suffering from leprosy. He was also the recipient of the Padma Vibhushan, the Gandhi Peace Prize, as well as the United Nations prize in the field of Human Rights.

Meeting and felicitating Baba Amte was a memorable moment and a great privilege for me.

At a seminar with Lioness president, Mrs. Vilas Lokhandwala, to honour Padma Shri Baba Amte for his work as a social reformer

PANDIT CHANDRAKANT

Pandit Chandrakantji

During Ajeet's illness, a well-meaning friend had sent an astrologer to meet us. *Pandit* Chandrakantji was a well-built, imposing person, who was over six feet tall and who possessed a strong personality. He had a thick mane of salt-and-pepper hair, which was usually covered with a black round cap. His forehead was always streaked with a vibrant vermillion *tilak*. Panditji was an accomplished astrologer and instilled a great deal of confidence in Ajeet. He became a big support for us throughout this period and later kept visiting our home, more as a friend than as an astrologer.

His support continued even after my husband's passing. When I began attending office, his astrology and advice was a big help, especially when I had to deal with difficult Delhi-based clients who were not paying us our dues. He even foresaw a period during which money would be slipping through my fingers. Since this would be inevitable, he advised that I invest in an upcoming property, which I could pay off in instalments while the property was being built on. This way, the money would still go out of my hands, as my chart indicated, but in the long run would prove to be a valuable investment.

Over the years, I saw Panditji transition from a reputed astrologer to the spiritual head of an ashram. He told me during this time that, one night in a dream, he had been instructed to build a temple to Ma Tulja Bhavani at Brij Bhumi (the lands associated with Lord Krishna) in a place through which a river was flowing. This dream created a strong urge in Panditji and sent him scouting in all directions for land on which to build his dream temple. Finally, the land he identified was a spot in Vrindavan in Mathura (the birthplace of Lord Krishna in Uttar Pradesh), a place with the River Yamuna flowing through it.

To commence construction, he sold off his plot of land in South India to pay for the land at Vrindavan. Then, with a great deal of hard work as well as generous donations from his clients and well-wishers, he was able to build a beautiful temple to Ma Tulja Bhavani. He also became the guru of an ashram that he established in the same place.

The ashram, which has a *goshala*, conducts daily yagnas and *bhandaras*. During one of his last visits to see us, Panditji informed me that when he was diagnosed with cancer, he stayed at the ashram. His cancer was cured, and he was convinced this was thanks to the daily walks he would take in front of the goshala, with the *gomatas* watching him with benevolent eyes.

I was happy and grateful that he attended the launch of my first book in February 2000. At the launch, he mentioned to my guru, *"Santosh ben mein himmat hai, yeh kitaab likhne ke liye."* ("Sister Santosh has shown courage in bringing out this book.")

Panditji passed away in 2014. His ashram* is well worth a visit if one happens to visit Vrindavan.

* Shree Sarveshwari Ma Tulja Bhavani Trust. 111 Godhulipuram Shreedham, Vrindavan, Mathura (UP) 281121. Mobile No.: 7666678686, 9323960898

PREMJI: THE RAM BHAKT

Premji

It was in 1983 that a dear friend of mine, named Usha, introduced us to her guru, Shri Prem Nath Sethi, also known as Premji. He was the disciple of Swami Satyanandji Maharaj of Ramasharnam, New Delhi. Premji was an embodiment of love. Whoever came to him, he would press that person's feet or shoulders. He was very gentle with Ajeet when he found out about his illness, and he was the one who suggested I recite a *Ram mantra* to cope with the situation. I am sure that reciting the Ram mantra, along with the Shiva japa, gave me added strength. The Ram mantra became internalised after a time, and one of these mantras would always be going on within me.

After Ajeet passed away, I began to feel it was no longer appropriate to recite both the mantras. I wrote to Premji, informing him that I was going back to reciting only my Shiva mantra. Somehow, I did not feel the need to recite the Ram mantra anymore. I was surprised when he wrote back to say that I should continue with the Ram mantra. I was in a quandary and asked for guidance before going to sleep. That night, I had a dream in which I was at the Ramasharnam ashram. I was walking away, and Premji caught hold of my arm and insisted that I don't leave. I somehow managed to pull myself away and walk out. The dream provided me some relief. The mantra had given me a great support and strength, but at the same time, I felt it had achieved its purpose. The understanding of the Ram mantra and why Premji gave it to everyone who came to him dawned on me some twenty years later.

I never knew the significance of the Ram mantra until I heard another sage say that it is the most powerful mantra. God can be found in the mantra of Ram.

Contemplating on this, I understood that *Ra* stands for the Sun and that the *m* in Ram stands for the Moon. The three most vital aspects of Creation on the physical plane are the life force (*prana*), cosmic mind (*manas shakti*), and consciousness (*atman*), which are part of Cosmic Consciousness (*Paramatman*).

The *Ra*, or Sun, is represented by the *pingala nadi*, through which the Sun's energy flows and which is what contributes to the life force. The *m* represents the *ida nadi*, through which the Moon's energy flows. One is the source of cosmic prana, and the other is the source of the cosmic mind. In order for Consciousness to manifest on the physical plane, it requires support of the universal prana (the life force), as well as the cosmic mind. For this, first a subtle grid is created, which is comprised of nadis and *chakras*. As mentioned earlier, the main nadis are pingala to channel the solar energy and ida to channel the lunar energy. The third main central nadi, or *sushumna*, acts as the pathway for the free flow of consciousness.

Nisargadatta Maharaj, in his book, *Self Knowledge and Self Realisation*, puts the Ram mantra into a clearer perspective. He writes the following:

> Consider the power of the bisyllabic word *Rama* that rests in perfection. *Mara* means fear; but just reverse the syllables, and what a difference it makes! When the rhythm (Rama) is stopped, one is dead. But one who is mad after it (Rama mantra), experiences the status of perfection and witnesses the disappearance of the whole universe along with its paraphernalia. The two syllables *Ra-ma* have imprisoned the cosmic power in the interior of an atom.

My understanding of what Maharaj is saying is that the Ram mantra, when practiced diligently, brings balance to the two hemispheres of the brain. The channels are cleared of mental and emotional blocks, and the energy flows freely through the sushumna. Through this mantra, one can attain a state of *samadhi*, wherein one can experience the state of Wholeness and the disappearance of all form. Thus, it becomes a suitable and safe mantra for everyone.

OUR PET JEFFREY

In October 1984, my sister Raj called up one morning and told me that there was someone who wanted a home for a three-week-old pup. She then asked whether I would like to have it as a pet for the children. I think it was October 8 when we got the miniature dachshund pup at our home. Shibani named him Jeffrey after Jeffrey Archer, her favourite author at that time.

Jeffrey came as a blessing. He was a beautiful pup, a source of joy and a welcome distraction from the vacuum that had been left

Jeffrey sitting on his favourite chair

in our lives by Ajeet's passing in September 1984. Jeffrey became an integral part of our lives. A very sensible little pup, he did not mess around the house and did his business either in the toilet or when he went out for a walk. His playful side would come to the fore once Gautam came home from school and took off his shoes. He would often keep an alert watch on Gautam at this time, and as soon as Gautam took one sock off, Jeffrey would snatch it and run away. What would follow was a race around the house to retrieve it from him.

When I sat for my evening prayers, he would come and sit right next to me until I had completed my puja. This habit of his continued even after group meditation started in our flat. He would then go and sit next to Justice M. L. Dudhat who was our Guru leading the meditation. Once the Om was chanted, signifying the end of the silent meditation session after thirty minutes, he would quietly slink away.

He was my companion on morning walks at the Marine Drive promenade, which was just a few minutes' walk from our home. I did not have to put him on a leash once we had crossed the road and had gotten onto the footpath. Even though he was tiny, he would not hesitate to challenge a big dog. Seeing his size, the bigger dogs perhaps realised his bark was more than his bite, so they would just give an indulgent glance and move on.

He brought unbounded joy to our lives for seventeen years, a ripe old age for a dog. When he first came to us, we had been informed by the Kennel Club that as his pedigree went back almost twelve generations, he would be a very healthy dog.

One day, a year or so after his passing, one of my friends, who is a clairvoyant, came to visit me. To my surprise, while sipping a cup of tea, she mentioned that she could see Jeffrey sitting quietly under the table.

MEETING SWAMI RAMA

In 1986, I read Swami Rama's best-known book, *Living with the Himalayan Masters*. The book was fascinating; he carries the reader through the different stages of his life with the Himalayan masters. It reminded me of *Autobiography of a Yogi* by Swami Yogananda, which I had read when I was in college.

It was during my visit to our Delhi branch office in August 1988 that I came to know that Swami Rama was at his ashram in Rishikesh. I informed Meena, and she flew down from Bombay. The next morning, we hired a taxi and drove to Rishikesh, a trip which took close to seven hours. We were very excited, but the excitement was, however, short-lived. On reaching the ashram, we were told that Swamiji had left for Delhi in the morning. The attendant was considerate enough to serve us some refreshments, and noting down Swamiji's address in Delhi, we did a turnaround and headed back.

On reaching the outskirts of Delhi around six o'clock in the evening, we decided to look for the address in Greater Kailash. We arrived, looking quite bedraggled and tired. We rang the doorbell, and the door was opened by a young lady, who may have been Swamiji's secretary. She enquired about the purpose of our visit, and on being told that we had come to see Swami Rama, she wanted to know whether we had an appointment with him. We replied in the negative. While we were conversing with her, a tall and handsome man, dressed in a maroon robe with his neck-length hair combed back, crossed from one room to another not far from where we were standing. Seeing us, he asked the lady what the discussion was about. She told him the purpose of our visit and also that we didn't have an appointment with him.

Swamiji very graciously invited us in, and we sat on a sofa opposite him. We then told him we had gone to visit him at his ashram in Rishikesh but were informed by the attendant that he had left in the morning. He offered us tea with some snacks and then, since it was getting late, we asked him if we could come the next day. He said we could come at eight in the morning. Meena and I looked at each other; we were already scheduled to visit the Chhatarpur Temple. Swamiji saw us hesitating and asked, "How about 9 a.m.?" It was thus decided that we would come to meet him at that time the next day.

Early next morning, we went to Chhatarpur, a huge complex of temples dedicated to different deities. The main temple there is dedicated to the devi. When bowing down before the deity, the pandit blesses devotees with a cone-shaped silver *topi*. Much later, during the course of my spiritual journey, I experienced chakras over my head in the same shape. The illustration on the next page of this experience is from my book *Kundalini Diary,* the second book in *The Kundalini Trilogy*.

I could only understand the subtle significance of receiving the blessing from the pandit after my spiritual experience that was to follow years later. The blessing enhanced the spiritual unfoldment of an individual, as and when the time was right. I marvel at the wisdom of the sages who have devised ways and means to nudge human consciousness along the way toward enlightenment—the ultimate goal of a human incarnation.

January 9, 1996

I see a crown of chakras on my head. They rotate in different directions.

Looking back, I notice that until now, I was drawing a complete head of my figure in meditation. Now, the heads are open at the top, signifying a fully operating *sahasrara chakra*.

The divinity of my guru is brought to my knowledge time and again.

The drawing as it appeared in my second book *Kundalini Diary*, 36–37

Our primary interest to visit Chhatarpur was to meet the Baba of Chhatarpur, the resident sage and head of the complex. He was a renowned and powerful *tantric*, who was often visited by politicians. We visited all the temples, and when we were finished, we walked down the steps to the lower level of the complex, where we came across a line of people waiting for Baba's darshan. The line did not seem to be moving, and when we checked with an attendant, he said that it was not the time for darshan. Despite this update, we decided to look for Baba and try to find him in the complex. We went peeping into the rooms of the living quarters, until we suddenly found ourselves in a room where Baba was standing, with his arms resting on a trolley and talking to another man. It was obvious we had barged into a meeting of sorts. We were taken aback by the unexpected shock of the encounter and could not utter any words except to join our hands respectfully. He looked up and without displaying any surprise, asked, *"Kahan say aaye ho?"* This meant, "Where have you come from?" Taken off guard by the sudden query, I blurted out, *"Upar se..."* This meant, "from above." He then shook his head and said he was busy at the moment. Then, he added something to the effect that he was not well. He called an attendant and asked him to take us into the next room and give us refreshments. After we had partaken of them, we went back and thanked him. What I remember of Baba is his glance. When he looked into my eyes, I felt that he was seeing not only my present but my past and future as well.

Later, we returned to Swami Rama's ashram in Delhi to keep our appointment with him. I did not have any matter to discuss, as such. When we reached the ashram, Swamiji met us in his study. He showed us a line of bookshelves, full of his books. There was a *veena* or a *sitar* lying next to him. Meena was engaged in a conversation with him, and I sat listening. I heard him tell Meena,

"If you tell me at what time you are meditating, I will guide you." It was a passing statement that stayed with me for some reason. Then he turned his attention to me. His first question to me was, "Are you *Sikh*?" I thought he was asking me if I was sick, so I told him, "No, Swamiji, I am not sick." Then he asked about my family. On learning that I had three young children and a family business to look after, he remarked, "You have many responsibilities. There's still time." He left it at that, and I did not even think of asking him, "Time for what?"

We left after spending a good amount of time with him, having him totally to ourselves. I did not have any further personal contact with Swami Rama except through his books.

The memory of my encounter with Swami Rama surfaced when Sant Dharmanandji, a direct disciple of Swami Rama, was visiting Mumbai in December 2016. He had come for the launch of his book, *Mystic Experiences with the Himalayan Masters.* Santji had also been in touch with my son, Gautam, earlier, who now invited Santji home for an evening meal. It was a pleasant surprise to see a bubbly, clean-shaven head young man dressed in a crisp, white *kurta-pyjama* walk in with a bouquet in his hands. He met us with a big hug. I shared my experience of Swami Rama with him, and he shared with us some wonderful stories and miracles that took place in the presence of Swami Rama, who enfolded us in his loving energy field during Santji's narration.

Our discussion brought back my memory of what I assume was an experience of *shaktipat*. I mentioned this in my book *Kundalini Diary*:

March 1, 1996

12:30 a.m.—Shaktipat: Dreaming while only half asleep is a powerful experience. I am outside Swami Rama's study in Delhi, listening to Swamiji playing his sitar inside. I can hear a bird chirping. Something inside me starts fluttering. Suddenly, without any warning, there is a loud sound, like a thunderclap. My body is blown to smithereens, disintegrated completely. I am out of a body that is left feeling totally lifeless and breathless. For weeks after this experience, I would hear a loud burst like a firecracker, going off in my head. It would happen at unexpected times, such as when I was lying in bed reading. Guruji tells me that it represents the destruction of my past *karmas*. At some point, this curious sound stopped of its own accord.

In his book *Kundalini Yoga: In Search of the Miraculous (Volume 1)*, Osho similarly writes the following:

> ...there are only two ways of hammering the kundalini. And the third way is an extraordinary way—the way of shaktipat, or transmission of energy. This is an astral way, and it needs a medium, a vehicle...You can be your own medium, but initially it can be dangerous. The shaktipat, the fallout of energy, can be so powerful that you may not withstand it. It is just possible that some delicate senses of your body are jammed, or they break down...The medium of another person serves as an instrument regulating the energy in its relation with your capacity to withstand it...No one can do shaktipat, but someone's presence can catalyse it, cause it to happen.

Osho, *Kundalini Yoga: In Search of the Miraculous* (Volume 1)

The diary entry (left) supported by the drawing as it appeared in my second book *Kundalini Diary*, 90–91

It was wonderful spending an evening with Santji. It was an evening that was full of intimate anecdotes, one that left all of us feeling we had met before even though we hadn't. Nothing happens unless it is ordained, and I feel blessed for being reminded that we are always being watched and taken care of, as and when required. I stay forever in gratitude for these reminders.

Santji, in his wisdom and love, continues to give me guidance for my good health.

With Sant Dharmananda at my residence in 2016

CLOSURE OF DELHI OFFICE

It was around 1990 that the Delhi branch office incurred heavy losses. The general manager, who was a lady, had not been collecting dues from a client who was in the lottery business and who had advertised heavily in newspapers from the north. She kept reassuring us by saying the client would pay us soon. The situation was becoming unmanageable as she was always coming up with some excuse or the other on behalf of the client. I went to Ajeet's friends for their advice. Their suggestion was that I go to Delhi with two letters—one asking for her resignation and the other terminating her services in case she did not offer to resign. I was nervous as she was quite an aggressive woman and well settled in her role as the boss of our Delhi branch. Ajeet had left blank, signed cheque books with her. He had trusted her, and as a result, she had a free hand with the company's cash.

Thus started my journey venturing into avenues I had never in my wildest dreams thought I would enter. To cut a long story short, I flew down to Delhi and called Aradhana (name changed). When I mentioned that I was in Delhi, she asked whether it was a visit for business or pleasure. I told her it was business and that she should come by eleven in the morning to the hotel. When I gave the letters to her, she was shocked and angrily said the agency was her baby and that she would take the matter to court.

The real drama started after that. As no help was coming from her, our focus shifted to collecting the money directly from the lottery client. However, he said he only recognised Aradhana and would not deal with anyone else. Whenever I would visit the client's office to ask for our dues, I would be surprised to see that Aradhana would be sitting by his side. We now had no doubt that both of them were in this together and that they seemed to have worked out some arrangement between themselves.

Ajeet's friend Prem Khanna, the one who had stood as the bank guarantor earlier, said that it was not advisable for me to visit the client alone. I was very grateful that Prem accompanied me whenever I went for the meetings with the lottery client. He was a good support, and he was able to talk with him man to man. The client gave dates as to when he would start paying our dues in instalments. These were false promises. He then started harassing my accounting department, asking for clarifications where none were required on old bills as well as on all details that had been submitted earlier. Then he went on to deny that he had asked for the ads to be released.

Seeing the hopelessness of the situation, our lawyers suggested we file a case against the client. We also took the advice of a senior judge, who was very clear that filing a case would not yield any results and that I would have to try other means to recover the dues.

"What other means could I adopt?" I asked my chartered accountant, who was present at the meeting. He explained to me that the best option would be to use muscle. I didn't know what that meant. He then asked me to go meet someone called Jagga Pehlwaan (name changed) in Delhi. He went by the suffix of *pehlwaan*, which means "a wrestler."

Back in Bombay, one of Ajeet's close friends gave me some

understanding of the role of Jagga Pehlwaan as "a godfather." I asked him whether I would have to offer a percentage of the dues to Jagga Pehlwaan, and he said I was not to worry about that at this stage. He told me the name of Ajeet's friend who could arrange for me to meet this so-called godfather.

The next day, I went over to this friend's residence and explained the situation to him. He was pretty cool about the whole thing and said when he would be visiting Delhi next, I could also go with him, and we would see how this situation could be worked out.

The next day came, and I was introduced to a sardarji, who held some post at a prestigious club. Ajeet's close friend told me the sardarji would take me to meet this godfather. One day, I got a call saying that the meeting was fixed for eleven in the morning. I started getting butterflies in the stomach and took a pill to relax my nerves. I met the sardarji at a restaurant. He said that the godfather's office was around the corner, and we should walk there. We hardly walked for five minutes until we came to an entrance, where we found some steps leading up. We climbed about six steps to a landing with a table and a man sitting behind it with a twirled moustache and a revolver in his hands. I heard a voice in Hindi say, "Let them come." From that moment on, I became sort of like a robot, for I followed the voice without thinking, going further up a few steps before we came to an open door.

I walked in, oblivious to whether the sardarji had followed or not. I maneuvered myself into an ornate chair at a big ornamental glass table, beyond which was a man about fifty years of age, sitting on some kind of a throne. He was dressed in a cream-coloured silk kurta-pyjama, and around his neck was a thick gold chain with a big round pendant, which was studded with jewels. It was all quite overwhelming. A glass of juice was put in front of me, and I became aware of the sardarji and the godfather having a conversation. I had regained my composure and, addressing the godfather in Punjabi as *Praji*, went on to present my case. After hearing me out, he called the bodyguard in and asked him to get the lottery client. I was quite horrified at this turn of events and asked him why he was calling him now. His answer was simple. The matter should be settled then and there. Much to my relief, the gunman came back and said the client was not in his office.

The godfather then said he would let me know about the matter in a few days. Heaving a sigh of relief, I walked down and asked the sardarji to tell me more about Jagga Pehlwaan. What I understood was that political parties used his muscle. The room where we sat was nice and comfortable but if one went further in, there was supposedly a torture room. I don't know whether he was exaggerating. I voiced my fear to the sardarji about the client's reaction, as the client was apparently a kind of mafia don himself. He told me that no one would touch me once they knew I was under the godfather's protection.

In the evening, I narrated the entire episode to Prem Khanna. He was impressed that I had the courage to go and meet the mafia. I said I had no choice, else our ship would sink due to the huge outstanding debt we were in. He wanted to know my impression of the godfather. I told him my impression of the man, after overlooking the ostentatiousness of his office, was that behind it all he seemed to be clean and gentle. There was nothing in his persona that came across as threatening. He had put me at ease such that I had been able to speak my mind. At one end, I was feeling heroic and, at the other end, fearful, not knowing what I had gotten myself and my children into. My sister-in-law was horrified and cautioned me not to tell anyone that I had gone and met Jagga Pehlwaan.

After a few days, my accountant, who happened to be sitting in the lottery client's office at the time to collect some cheques, called me to say that an aggressive-looking *goonda* had come into the office and was asking for the client. On another line, the client's operator called me and shouted at me, telling me to call back the goonda I had sent. I told him that I had not sent anyone. I heard a loud thud, and the line got cut. I panicked and called the godfather and asked him not to use brute force by sending ruffians. He replied that these things are not done gently. After saying this, he hung up the phone. My accountant, who was shaking a bit from the experience, came back and sketched out the scenario to me. He reported that the goonda had been waiting to meet the client for quite a while, and after he had waited long enough, he got up and strode to the client's cabin, kicked open the door, and made the client call the godfather at knifepoint.

The feeling in me was that a war had started. The godfather called and said I could go and collect my cheques the next day. I was excited, and on receiving confirmation from the client's office, Prem accompanied me there. The client was okay, though he complained that it was not right of me to adopt these methods. He gave me postdated cheques and said he would give the balance in due course. However, only a few of those cheques cleared. About 90 percent of the money remained outstanding.

Back in Bombay, one of Ajeet's friends dropped by at the office after he came to know about my husband's passing. He was curious to know how I was managing. He became concerned when I mentioned the situation to him, and said if I went to Delhi again, I should put myself under the protection of someone whom he called Vicky (name changed), who held a position in the Research and Analysis Wing (RAW) of India's intelligence agency. I was told I could address him as Vicky *bhaiya*. I did just that when I was next in Delhi and was invited to Vicky's house, where I met Vicky bhaiya and his sister. He wanted to know all the details about the lottery client, where exactly his office was, the details of the place in Delhi where I was staying, the people I met, our office location, and so on. All these questions seemed a little strange to me. Bhaiya was a very pleasant-looking and amiable person. In due course, he visited Bombay. Someone from the intelligence agency came to scout around my place, and after this, Vicky bhaiya came to see how I was doing.

Nothing much transpired after that. At the end of a fairly unfruitful attempt to collect our rightful dues, we decided to close the Delhi office. There was no way to meet the running expenses of the office after this setback. Aradhana had chosen to tender her resignation. We were informed by staff members that when Ajeet had passed away, she had put up a notice mentioning that the branch manager of the Bombay office had passed away. And this after all the trust Ajeet had placed in her.

A year or so later, I went to Delhi to attend a wedding and chanced to meet Jagga Pehlwaan at the reception. He enquired whether I had collected the full amount that was due to me. He was surprised and wondered aloud why I had not gone back to him when the cheques had bounced and payments had stopped. I did not tell him that the reason was that I had become quite apprehensive after hearing stories of the underworld. Another reason I kept concealed to myself was that Pandit Chandrakantji had called one day and had recommended I hold back on my efforts to recover the money owed to me. He had said he would be coming to see me. I was quite surprised as he did not voluntarily call to say he would be coming. He may have seen my astrological chart. He asked me not to push too hard for my dues for the next few months, as there could be repercussions, and it was not worth the risk to me and my children.

And so the chapter of the Delhi branch office came to an end, and life in Bombay resumed its usual course, with me attending office daily as before, hoping that we would eventually resolve this predicament. But it was a realisation at the time for me that the advertising business is a risky one.

THE GURU APPEARS: JUSTICE M. L. DUDHAT

Justice M. L. Dudhat

In August 1995, my friend Usha Banerji invited me to attend with her a weekly lecture series, called Mental Physics. The course was led by the Honourable Justice M. L. Dudhat of the Bombay High Court, near to our immediate neighbourhood on Marine Drive.

My life until this point had passed through a series of crisis-filled events for more than a decade, and I had confronted each major cataclysm with equanimity, even as cherished alliances fell through and relationships of mutual cooperation frayed at the edges. It had taken great effort to keep the business afloat after the death of my husband with the help of my brother, Shiv, even as

I single-handedly brought up three sensitive and gifted children. By now, my grown-up son had just taken over the reins of the company, and I found myself relatively at loose ends for the first time in my event-filled life. So I made a solemn resolve to attend the course lectures regularly from the very first day.

These lectures were being held every Wednesday at six in the evening. The title of the course sounded strange, and I had no interest in learning about physics. Sitting through the first lecture, I realised that the subject had more to do with the mind. The course book also had eight breathing exercises and affirmations* to be recited after each breath. I surprised myself by actually attempting to do the first breathing exercise at home. The breath and its companion affirmation had to be done daily as instructed, until the next breath was added to it as the course progressed. After practicing the breath for a couple of weeks, I realised that every morning I was looking forward to practicing it. I soon became aware of why this was. While reciting the affirmations, I was seeing things; in fact, I was looking in all directions. This was strange because my eyes were not open. As time went on, I became more and more attentive and was motivated to pen down and draw what I was seeing. This was an experience completely different from the ordinary.

I became more attentive during the lectures, observing the teacher and his persona. One could mistake him for a college professor or even a well-to-do businessman. He did not look at all like the stern judge who had sent criminals to the gallows during his long tenure of dispensing justice in the Bombay High Court. Soft-spoken, unassuming, mild-mannered, and very humble, there was nothing remarkable about him at first glance. He was always

---

* See Appendix B

a poised and good speaker while delivering the lectures week after week, which I heard he had been doing for the past thirteen years. The talks were in an everyday conversational tone, laced with subtle wit and illustrated with clear examples that help to deepen one's understanding. As I progressed through the course, I practiced the breaths and recited the affirmations, and the visualisations I saw in my mind became more and more fascinating. I felt as if I were Alice in Wonderland.

The foreword of the course book had a fascinating line in its affirmation: "The riddle of the Universe is about me, and I am now solving it." There was a hint of adventure in these words, something different from the mundane.

After completion of the first two breaths, I decided to bring my unusual experiences to the judge's notice. I waited after the lectures to show him my illustrations and notes. I did not know how to address him. Some people called him sir, others master, and a few others by his surname. The name for him that spontaneously came out of my mouth was Guruji. I was quite surprised as he did not look remotely like a guru to me. He possessed no flowing beard or ochre robes. Showing him my drawings, I mentioned that I wanted to know what was happening. He casually looked at the illustrations and handed them back saying, "It's okay. It happens." That was all he said, but it did not answer my question.

I stayed with my practice, and the phenomena continued. I needed answers to some of my questions. I called Guruji's residence and requested a meeting, since I wanted to understand what was happening while performing the breaths and meditations. He did not answer my questions. Instead he asked me whether I would like the process to stop. I thought for a moment and decided that I would like to continue the journey into the unknown.

Guruji then asked me a few questions, such as whether I had any young children, old parents, or in-laws to take care of. And finally he asked whether I had any fears. This question seemed to be important because the course book also says, "Do not doubt. Do not have fear. Have childlike faith."

Fortified by his instructions to continue with my practice, I started to pay serious attention to what was transpiring during the practice, as well as during my meditations. This marked the beginning of my incredible spiritual journey, which soon moved on to the next level.

Afterward, I often pondered over the statement about having a childlike faith. Having such faith was not a problem for me, for my inherent nature was one of trust. However, the words about not doubting and not fearing aroused my curiosity. What could there be to doubt and fear in a self-development course? In order to find out the answer to this question, I started the practice in all seriousness. In due course, I realised that in getting into the practice of the breaths, I had embarked on an inward journey for which there was no road map. Thus my attention moved from without and turned within into areas unknown. It was an adventure of another kind, which could be a cause for fear and doubt and hence caution.

REV. ALEX ORBITO: THE PSYCHIC SURGEON

Rev. Alex Orbito

Sometime in 1997, we heard that a psychic healer, Rev. Alex Orbito, had come from the Philippines to hold a two-day seminar at a hotel in Mumbai. Along with my children and a friend, I attended the seminar. We witnessed and experienced a psychic healing that was conducted in full public view on a projector's screen. We could see the healer plunge his fingers into an area of the body and come out with a black jelly-like substance, which he would then drop into a basket. His attendant would then take a piece of cotton and cleanly wipe the area of the patient's body that had been worked upon.

My turn came to go through the experience. I lay down on the table, and it felt like Rev. Orbito thrust his hand into my abdomen. I heard the sound of a splash, similar to the sound one hears when one thrusts one's hands into a bucket of water. I had gone into the experience with total awareness in order to observe and understand what was happening. He drew out a black jelly-like substance, and I saw him drop it into the basket below. The young lady attendant wiped my abdomen, and I got up to leave. I looked into the basket to see the jelly, but to my surprise, I saw nothing. Like this, Rev. Orbito healed a number of people over two days.

On the second day, the first half of the session was dedicated to questions and answers. I asked what had happened to the black jelly that had been dropped into the basket. He answered that it was subtle matter that had congealed and, which when released, evaporates and gets absorbed into the atmosphere and its elements.

Rev. Orbito also made us do some exercises to bring the body back into a certain balance. Somebody asked him whether, once healed, the cured problem could arise again. His answer was that if it was a strong *karmic* problem, it may not be healed. Otherwise, the person would get healed and would stay free of the problem as long as he or she did not repeat old patterns of emotion, mental thought, and behaviour.

Having witnessed and experienced the healing, I could understand the process and authenticity of psychic surgery based on my own understanding of prana and the *pranamaya kosha.*

Being endowed with the gift of healing, Rev. Orbito could identify where the energy had congealed in an individual's pranamaya kosha. He would then pick out the black jelly-like substance that was creating a block and hindering the flow of prana in the subtle channels and which was consequently disturbing the flow of blood and oxygen to the physical nervous system. This lack of free flow of blood and oxygen, if not rectified, might ultimately lead to a health problem, most likely in the area where the energy had congealed.

I feel meditation is an effective way of dissolving energy blocks. This is not an overnight process. Regular daily practice is required. Group meditations are also very effective, as the collective energy of the group enhances the vibrations. Being under the guidance of an experienced teacher is important. Over time, our thought processes change, energy flow is enhanced, and the blocks in the nadis start to dissolve.

It was important to learn that the congealed energy in the pranamaya kosha affects the physical organs in the related area. Meditation is one way to cleanse the uprising of karmic issues that appear in our pranamaya kosha. It helps to either remove or reduce the *doshas* of past karmic issues. This it does by bringing balance into our mental and emotional states and into our interactions with others.

Paramahansa Yogananda, in his book *The Essence of Self-Realisation*, writes this about the same issue:

> "An important factor in overcoming karma is meditation. Every time you meditate, your karma decreases, for at that time, your energy is focused in the brain and burns up the old brain cells. After every deep meditation, you will find yourself becoming fresh inside."

A NEW KIND OF SEEING

In my meditations, I could see what could not be seen with physical eyes. I was disappointed at not being able to elicit any explanation from Guruji whenever these magical visions and experiences would unfold. On gently being told by him that these answers would all unfold in due course, I felt lost. Once I told Guruji, "I think my chakras are moving." He just said, *"Santoshji, in chakron ke chakron mein mat pado."* (This meant, "Santoshji, don't get entangled in the mesh of these wheels.") I felt that he didn't take my experiences seriously enough, but I doggedly persisted.

It was difficult to interact with Guruji on this subject, and I felt frustrated. Over time, it was during the sharing of our experiences after the group meditations that provided me with a sense of assurance. This ended my self-imposed isolation and to some extent ultimately resulted in validating my efforts and experience.

In his wisdom, Guruji remained passive during these discussions. He neither made any comments nor gave any explanations. My co-meditators usually laughed indulgently at what they thought were my fantastic outpourings. At that time, it was like interacting with my Self by talking aloud to clear my own thinking. I needed an audience, a listener. So I chose Guruji to be the listener. Of course, given the circumstances, I now realise that this was the best possible response from him, since any active intervention on his part in the process of my unfoldment would have most probably put a stop to the journey.

Continuing with my practice, I realised that it was more exciting to solve the riddle of my experience by myself because it gave me an enormous amount of energy and inspiration to keep on expanding my limitations—so that I find out more and understand more. It was up to me to sharpen my intuitive faculty, to investigate and to enquire, because my guru wanted me to experience the adventure and joy of discovering new horizons.

It took me years thereafter to get a firm understanding of the subtleties of the human body-mind organism. The insights I was getting were my own, and my own truth. I did not have to doubt and ask myself, "Have I really experienced this, or have I only imagined it? Or is this an illusion based on what I have been told, heard, or read?'

BRAHMA VIDYA:
KNOWLEDGE OF CREATION

The Mental Physics Course, referred to as *Brahma Vidya* in India, took about eight months to complete. As mentioned earlier, it comprised eight breathing exercises, each having its own relaxing affirmation to be recited after each breath. The course was mainly comprised of lectures and brief demonstrations of the exercises, which were performed later by students at their homes. After doing the breathing exercises and reciting the affirmations, they were advised to meditate. It was important to get into the breathing exercises gradually and in the given order as each exercise locked into the next one in a proper sequence.

I had always found it extremely difficult to sustain interest in any one subject for long, and to undertake meditation on a sustained basis seemed to be quite a daunting task. I began to feel apprehensive when I realised the level of commitment required on my part to attend the lectures, which took almost a year to complete. However, I must have undergone a dramatic personality change to become so deeply absorbed in the practice of Brahma Vidya; it became almost like an addiction.

As I started the course, I felt an inner compulsion to learn all the affirmations by heart, with the result that I was fluent in reciting all of them within a week's time. During the initial days, I would note down an affirmation on a scrap of paper, which I would take out and read while travelling to work and while going up and down the elevator and almost everywhere else. I was truly obsessed.

Following instructions to the very last letter, I gradually got accustomed to the breathing exercises and affirmations. The next step was to get into the process of meditation and of learning to be still. I learnt to sit in a cross-legged position on a cushion, with my knees slightly lower than the body and my spine absolutely straight.

This is a quote from the course book:

> 'You do not see the force that makes you breathe, but you know that you do breathe. In the practice of the course of Brahma Vidya exercises in breathing and meditation, we go to the place where that force resides in the silence…'[1]

I wanted to reach that "silence." But for that, I had to be prepared to make a sacred vow to myself that nothing would come in the way of my practice. I kept that vow. I did not move out of the city of Mumbai, nor did I miss a single lecture until the course was completed and I had a fair idea as to the direction in which I was heading.

As I proceeded, I came across this quote in the course: "Never fear regarding spiritual awakening and unfoldment."[2]

When I read this, I began looking beyond the seemingly simple words and decided to find out what was in sadhana that could be considered fearful. This was the second time I had come across the word *fear*. Earlier, another spiritual teacher had asked me, "Santosh, do you know what fear is?" I had said, "No, what is it?" He had laughed, and that was the end of the matter. At times, I may have felt apprehensive but never fearful. Here was the opportunity, I thought, to find out what this fear was and what "spiritual awakening" is on this journey.

---

1 Swami K. S. Ramanathan, *Mental Physics: Lectures and Lessons* (Bombay: Private Circulation, 1980), 22.

2 Ibid., 46.

KUNDALINI SHAKTI

It was now obvious that my whole being had awaited the practice of Brahma Vidya with great patience through all the vicissitudes of my life until it could wait no longer. As soon as I had taken the first breath in this meditation practice, an electric switch was turned on in my consciousness, clearing all the accumulated cobwebs and allowing the light to shine in. It seemed almost as though I were being given a quick run and revision of the process of *kundalini* arousal, which I had probably spent years of purification and penance in several past lives attaining. I say this because in this lifetime up till now, I had simply no idea what kundalini was. Nor had I read any book or article about it. This was also confirmed by the renowned Gagangiri Maharaj of Khopoli, Maharashtra in his commendation for my first book, *Conscious Flight into the Empyrean*.

There now appeared to be a great urgency about the revelation of the whole mysterious process. The exercises, affirmations, and instantaneous results of the new practice were awe-inspiring, bringing home an awareness about the hand of destiny in my life, as it ordained what was to become a whole new way of living from then on. The results of the practice were astonishingly rapid. The first two breathing exercises of the course released a sequence of visuals before I had even started the affirmations. Much to my delight and astonishment, I was transported to an altered state of consciousness, in which I found myself a witness to the play of

Gagangiri Yogashram
Laxminagar, Khopoli, Dist. Raigad,
Maharashtra 410 204.

Guru Purnima, 9 July 1998

The dream-like visions presented by Santosh Sachdeva in this book are very good, and they represent the blessings of the Masters to this generation. Tapasvis like Mahavatar Babaji, who have been engaged in ascetic practices for hundreds of years in the mountains in India, can thus enlighten any jiva. Yet there are hundreds of thousands of beings to choose from, and at least thousands of Sadhus who can be so blessed.

The reason for her being singled out for this honour is that she too has been a part of the stream of Sadhus life after life, and this is the culmination of her own punyakarma involving hundreds of years of sadhana. Every single atom of her body has become receptive to the teachings of the Masters, and this book is the result.

This is a rarest of rare occurences, a mahadurlabh yoga in the physical world. I suggest, therefore, that she diligently continue this practice to illustrate the workings of the Kundalini.

Param Pujya Swami Gagangirinath Maharaj

This is an English translation of the Marathi message given by Gagangiri Maharaj subtle forces upon the psychic energy centres in my etheric body, even as my physical body sat undisturbed in deep meditation.

My daily routine would start with doing a few exercises as shown in the class and with reciting the affirmations. Then I would sit down for meditation. This was to be done on all days, even as the weekly lectures and demonstrations proceeded in the classroom. Gradually, my life fell into a pattern of the following sequence: performing the breathing exercises, relaxing with the affirmations, meditating, going to the office, meditating again in the evening, and going to sleep at night. Meanwhile, I eagerly awaited the pre-dawn hours for yet another round of meditation. The exercises, affirmations, and the subsequent revelations resulting from this practice became an integral part of my life. Since my perception works best through visual imagery, the education began for me in the form of visuals.

The role that I was required to play was of meditating, watching, and recording. It became more like a game, an entertainment, which was something new, something strange, and something exciting. Unfamiliar energies had started flowing into me, and the gentle workings of the life force did not raise any undue curiosity or questions in me that otherwise could have proved obtrusive. I was totally engrossed in seeing and observing.

I have not had any formal training as an artist. Perhaps it was my exposure to creative work at the ad agency that came to my rescue. I found myself compelled after each session of exercises, affirmations, and meditations to sit still and draw out on paper the visions I saw in as authentic a form as possible. This period saw me totally self-absorbed in a fairly enjoyable process of seeing visions in meditation, making rough sketches and notes, and then proceeding to make the finished drawings. I drew some visuals with crayons on sheets of paper, while others were painted on canvas with acrylic paints.

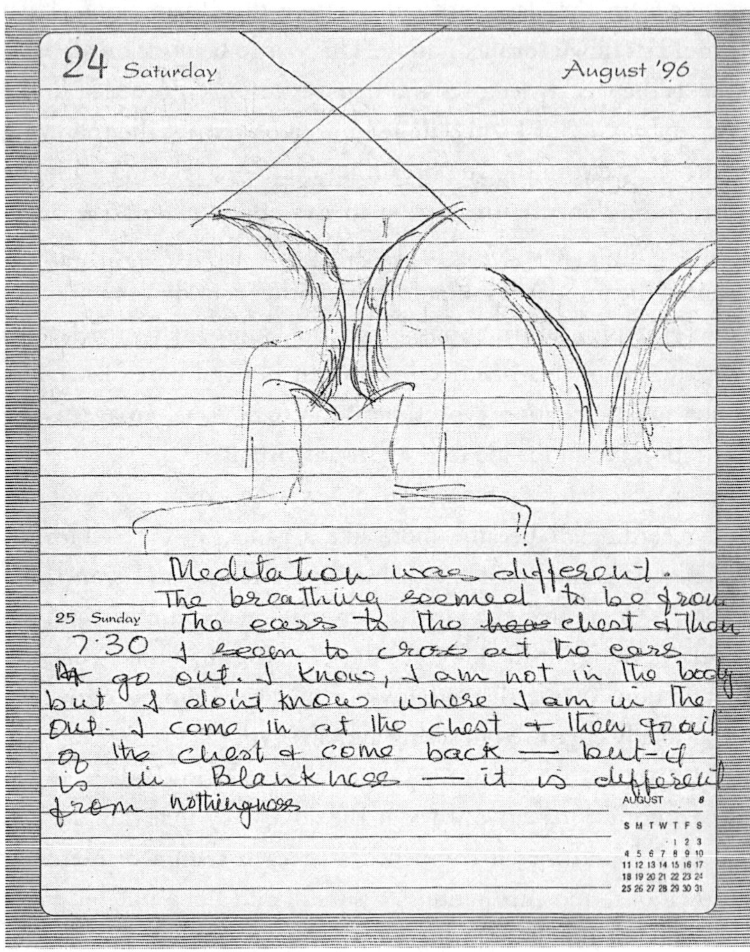

24 Saturday August '96

Meditation was different.
The breathing seemed to be from
the ears to the ~~hea~~ chest & then

25 Sunday

7:30 I seem to cross out the ears
& go out. I know, I am not in the body
but I don't know where I am in the
out. I come in at the chest & then go out
of the chest & come back — but it
is in Blankness — it is different
from nothingness

AUGUST 8

S	M	T	W	T	F	S
				1	2	3
4	5	6	7	8	9	10
11	12	13	14	15	16	17
18	19	20	21	22	23	24
25	26	27	28	29	30	31

Original diary entry and the finished drawing on facing page

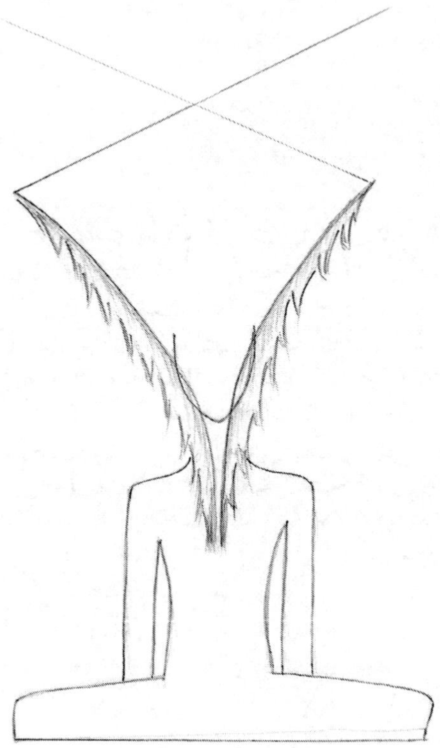

A u g u s t   2 4 ,   1 9 9 6

7:30 a.m.—The meditation is different. It seems as if I am breathing through my ears—but don't ask me how this is possible! The breathing is restricted to the area between the ears and the chest. I go out of the ears.

I know I am out of the body, but where? There is no sense of any presence. I know I am not in the body, but I don't know where I am outside either. I come in at the chest, go out from there, and come back, but it is in blankness—a feeling that is different from Nothingness. The breath is laboured. It seems as if I have wings.

The diary entry (left) supported by the final drawing as it appeared in my second book, *Kundalini Diary*, 190–191

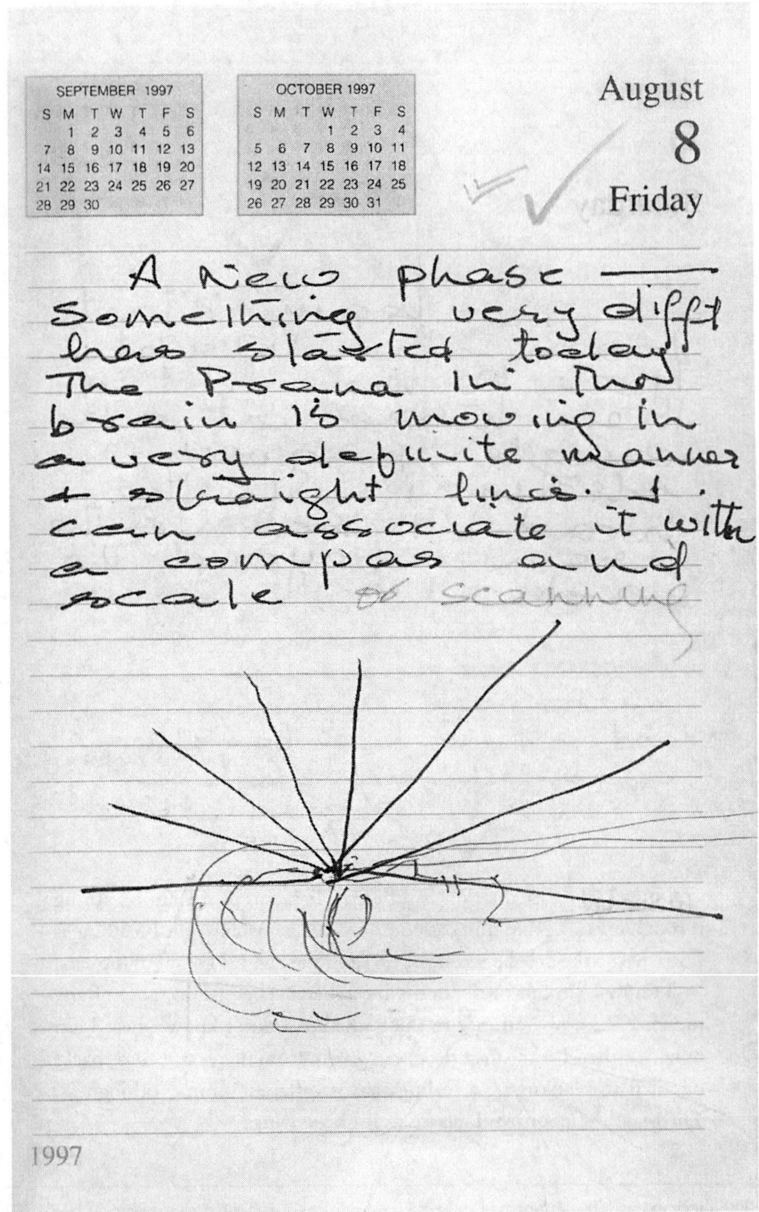

SEPTEMBER 1997

S	M	T	W	T	F	S
	1	2	3	4	5	6
7	8	9	10	11	12	13
14	15	16	17	18	19	20
21	22	23	24	25	26	27
28	29	30				

OCTOBER 1997

S	M	T	W	T	F	S
			1	2	3	4
5	6	7	8	9	10	11
12	13	14	15	16	17	18
19	20	21	22	23	24	25
26	27	28	29	30	31	

August
8
Friday

A New phase —
Something very difft
has started today.
The Prana in the
brain is moving in
a very definite manner
+ straight lines. I
can associate it with
a compass and
scale of scanning

1997

Original diary entry and the finished drawing on facing page

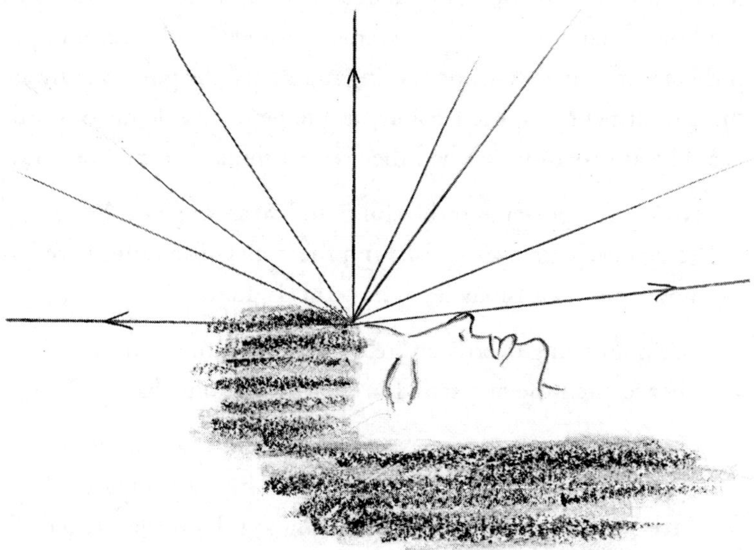

August 8, 1997

I have entered a new phase—there is a change in the flow and movement of prana. The energy projects out from the *ajna chakra* as a beam of light and moves in a very definite manner and in straight lines. The beam moves like a searchlight, starting the survey from over the head and moving in a downward arc.

The diary entry (left) supported by the final drawing as it appeared in my third book, *Kundalini Awakening*, 104–105

The process of observing and experiencing the visions on a sustained basis, day after day for more than three years, was made easy and smooth for me. A great deal of care and gentleness was evident, even when I had to be nudged and prodded or even when the chakras had to be manipulated. I presume this was done by the flow of energy, though it seems invisible hands are doing it. If there were any dark or unnerving moments, the guru was always there to dispel my apprehensions and to gently guide me onward.

The affirmation that had the greatest impact on me was this:

> 'I have the power and the ability to live as long as I desire,
> to achieve whatever I wish, and the doors of my mind are
> now open that I may learn how this is done.'

Without being overtly aware of it, my subconscious mind had already accepted the fact stated in the affirmations that

> 'I am the master of my own life! I will do what I desire to
> do…I rejoice! I did not feel this before, but now I know it!
> I feel with all the power of my being that I am the master
> of my own life—and I will begin now to truly live it.'

My own imagination, the creative faculty that is "a part of the infinite creative faculty of that power which we call God,"[1] started to actualise my thoughts and affirmations.

---

[1] Ramanathan, *Mental Physics: Lectures and Lessons*, 24.

THE INNER JOURNEY

Looking back upon my practice of the breathing exercises and affirmations that led to the visions, I believe these practices helped me to develop the "no-mind," or mindless, meditative state some refer to in the meditation movements. The ensuing visions I experienced now were more finely honed, and my interpretations of them became more holistic. This happened because the rational left brain and the emotional right brain in me had come into a state of balance. The empowered affirmations now became the road map that would guide me in my endeavour to find out, "Who am I?" "Where have I come from?" and "Where am I going?" Each word and thought presented itself in the form of a vision, whether within or without me. That is, each vision depended upon a particular thought or word as a stimulus.

In a previous lifetime, I had probably completed my sadhana to the level where I had begun the opening of my ajna chakra. It has been said that we start our spiritual evolution from where we left the body in our previous lives. In this lifetime, when the time was right, the full awakening of my ajna chakra helped me visually to revise my earlier sadhana and purification of my subtle body in order to continue and complete my spiritual journey.

I came to this understanding when I read in Lansdowne Zachary's book, *The Chakras and Esoteric Healing*; that the *swastik* symbol appears when the chakra has reached its final stage of development. It is fully charged, open, active, and energised by the awakened kundalini. This enables the chakra to perform all its functions efficiently. I was rather amazed that the swastik manifested in front of my eyes at the very beginning of my practice. As soon as it appeared, I could visualise a rapid purification of the chakras.

The first chakra that became active when I began meditating was the *manipura chakra*. What I saw here in my lower psychic centre was a thick, black, sticky, toxic prana moving out of the navel. This process continued until slowly and steadily a more clear prana flowed in the chakra. Once the heavy toxic prana became light, the dormant kundalini lying in the manipura chakra was released and moved upwards, taking with it the residual toxins of the manipura, *anahata*, *vishuddhi* chakras and then moving up through the ajna. It threw them out of the sahasrara chakra at the crown in the form of ashes and fireballs.

The foundation had been laid for the next phase of my growth on the path. Body, mind, intellect, and chakras—all were taken through the process of thorough cleansing, purification, and fine-tuning, including the chakras above the sahasrara.

With the opening up of all the chakras, I saw in my awareness a large expanse of water and a drop falling into it. As the drop touched the water, a ripple was created, and the drop disappeared. Simultaneously, the understanding I gained was that the expanse of water is the ocean, symbolising Consciousness as a whole. I also ascertained that the drop of water symbolises the individual consciousness, which, when its role is over, merges into Pure Consciousness, God, or Source.

Once the basic understanding was received, the ajna chakra became active, and I could feel the vibrations of the right and left hemispheres of the brain rotating at a certain speed in front of my

November 27, 1998

I see myself at the end of a long silver thread, hanging like a drop. In due course, I disengage from the thread and plonk! I fall into the ocean, creating ripples. This marks the merging of the individual consciousness with the Cosmic Consciousness.

The drawing as it appeared in my third book *Kundalini Awakening*, 196–197 forehead. The journey now started in earnest, and there seemed to be a sense of urgency to it.

As soon as my attention turned within, I became a witness to the movements of prana, chakras, and kundalini. The colourless flow of kundalini and prana were the same, the only difference being that the prana coming in with the inhalation was lighter and finer in texture than the prana moving out with the exhalation.

One day, I, as consciousness, entered the flow of prana to witness its cycle of movement within the nadi system of the body and outside of it. Prana, as the terrestrial manifestation of life-giving solar energy, revealed to me its perpetual cyclic motion outward from within. I found that it was all around, and it was a misty-looking substance. I also saw it as light. I saw it going in and out of the body, as if the body were just an integral part of the landscape. As I progressed in the meditations, my understanding also correspondingly improved. As my consciousness travelled to different vibratory levels, I discovered that the prana varies in its quality and density.

So, as stated earlier, the revelations I received were in the form of visions. As days passed, I was shown different visuals signifying different states of meditation. Once my body and mind got accustomed to the process that was taking place, the next step involved a further activating of the chakras, and this process continued through the subsequent stages. To sum it up, while I was meditating, I was given the gift to see the process of personal spiritual unfoldment in a vividly graphic and colourful portrayal. Like Sanjaya, who had the gift of *divya-drishti* (he could see events at a distance happening right in front of him, so he was able to narrate the action in the climactic battle of *Mahabharat*), I was given the ability to see what could not be seen by physical eyes. I was also given the sensitivity to see, feel, and experience the magnetic fields at different vibratory levels.

Chakras and the Body Temple*

1 – Muladhara (Base chakra)
2 – Svadhisthana (Sacral chakra)
3 – Manipura (Navel chakra)
4 – Anahata (Heart chakra)
5 – Vishuddhi (Throat chakra)
6 – Ajna (Brow chakra)
7 – Sahasrara (Crown chakra)

**This chart showing the location of the seven main chakras in the etheric body is a stylized version created by the author, and the colours and symbols shown here do not necessarily correspond to the descriptions in the traditional literature on kundalini.*

The drawing as it appeared in all three books of *The Kundalini Trilogy*

It all seemed too easy and too good to be true. All that was required of me was to do the exercises, recite the affirmations, state what I wanted to achieve, and the rest was going to be done for me. I stated my intention clearly and precisely, "Please lead me to my Source." I wanted to get acquainted with the very Source of my being. Things began to happen, and I became aware of an inner world completely unknown to me before. The onset of light and the cosmic energy that I experienced as the result of the exercises and affirmations was like the force of a solid, massive wall pushing against me. The exercises were accompanied with a high frequency sound, which was now a constant in my meditations, the quality of which changed as I shifted to a different vibratory level. Subsequent experiences gave a clear indication of my aptitude for perceiving abstract forms and committing them to paper with a rare artistic skill and with a hitherto unknown eye for detail.

I now understand that, without being fully aware of it, I have always engaged in a conversation with God, clearly stating my intent before starting any new venture. More often than not, the turn of events has been in the nature of a response from the Universe. I can surmise that my request, "Please lead me to my Source," brought on the profound vision of the *jiva* in the form of the individual drop falling into and merging with the Ocean of the Absolute.

Eventually, these conversations with God changed into mental conversations with my guru, following an episode of apprehension about being overwhelmed by the kundalini force. At that time, my guru had said to me with full assurance, "Think of me, and I will be there." I took him at his word, and from then on I found that all doubts, apprehensions, and worries were set to rest whenever I invoked the guru during a particularly rough passage of events.

Initially, I did not realise that the visions meant anything in particular or that they defined a certain awakening. Neither Guruji nor any of my friends took me seriously enough to help me understand what was happening. There soon came a stage when all the visions were just a bit too much for a novice to handle, especially after I realised through my random readings that I was going through a profound process of kundalini awakening. Guruji until then had only casually glanced at my drawings, not giving them much attention. However, I had come to realise that whatever it was that I was going through, it had to be taken seriously.

I also began to feel that I was on this path for good. If I wished to back off, the time was now. Later on in life, such a decision seemed to me like asking the pilot of an aircraft to stop midair to let me get off.

THE GENTLE FORCE

Within three months of attending the lectures on Brahma Vidya, doing the exercises, and recording the visions, everything else in my life had become unimportant. I was overseeing, but I was not involved in what was happening around me. My life was suddenly rendered too mechanical, too automatic, and I functioned with a robot-like efficiency that I found rather alarming.

I have always been a detached person, passing through the charted journey more as an observer than as an active subject of the vicissitudes of karma. For the first time in my life, I found something that held my interest so completely. But to my chagrin, I discovered that this new obsession was taking me away from my relationships.

Once I could admit clearly to myself how much the meditations had begun to mean to me and that I didn't wish to discontinue them at all, I decided to take matters firmly in hand in order to create a more balanced way of living. I had to reinvent my previous outgoing self. Once again, I started interacting with friends and also taking a greater interest in my relationships with those around me.

One wise friend was initially worried that my sudden obsession with occult texts had led me into hallucinating. This particular misconception of hers was over once I showed her some of my illustrations for the first time, almost six months into my meditations. She was very impressed with the artistic quality of the drawings, and she realised that whatever the motivating force behind this curious obsession, it was much more than mere hallucinations suffered by me. I found her a very sympathetic confidante from then on, one who often gave me special insights from the Hindu *Puranas* and *Shastras*, something that I knew very little about.

A strange comradeship had developed with my inner Self, whereby I was led to particular books containing lucid passages that described precisely what I had personally witnessed earlier while meditating. Over three years, I went through this process of self learning, of understanding in theory what I was experiencing in daily practice. I would go to a bookshop to browse around for something that might interest me. Whenever I picked up a pertinent book, there would be a faint, high-pitched whine in the right ear, a supernatural indication that the book contained material that would provide a solid framework for understanding my current encounters in meditation.

Thus began an adventure of solving the riddle of the visions I saw. I came to the conclusion that I was being transmitted a very fascinating pictorial insight into the theoretical knowledge of *Kundalini Yoga*. I realised that the Brahma Vidya Course had translated itself to give me the experience and knowledge of Kundalini Yoga.

It seemed as if I was being shown the visuals so that the theory given in several books by the masters of yore could be illustrated and described in a modern idiom. I firmly believe that the visuals have been given for a definite purpose, most probably to make it easier for new aspirants to understand the seemingly abstruse descriptions of Kundalini Yoga and to take away the fear of ridicule and madness commonly associated with it.

Kundalini, before I experienced Her, was just a word with awe-inspiring connotations. Somewhere in my subconscious mind was registered the knowledge that She was not to be tampered with and that it was best to let Her lie low in the very depths at the base of the spine. It was certainly not the sort of thing toward which one could develop a playful attitude, especially not without a guru's active supervision. If out of mere curiosity She was let loose upon the organism, the resulting energy could destroy the delicate physical and mental apparatus. As I started on my meditation, I slipped into the process of kundalini arousal very naturally and smoothly, not realising that I was headed towards a realm that only a few enter without trepidation.

I now understand that the Kundalini introduced Herself to me with grace and a rare gentleness. She treated my mind and body with incredible care.

In stark contrast to the writings of many aspirants, my experience underscores the love, the effulgent beauty, the gentleness, and the glory of the Mahashakti Kundalini unveiling Herself for ordinary human perception. In fact, I have found myself blessed to be in daily communion with this gentle cosmic force residing within me. She has made me aware of a special source for the feelings of tenderness, loving care, and affection, which are available from Her in a depth and quantity not possible in ordinary human interaction. I also wish to point out that my experience has been most unlike many authors who stress the aspect of intensified sexual arousal as an intrinsic part of the kundalini awakening. Almost none of the visuals, emotions, and physical sensations I received had anything even remotely connected to the lower vibratory levels of sexual desire.

My instances of apprehension came when the energy took on the form of a rotating dark bowl in my abdomen, causing a sensation of churning there. This sensation was accompanied with the deep roar of an electric dynamo. Whenever this sensation started, I would find myself clutching my abdomen with entreaties to stop, usually along with hurried invocations to not only the Hindu gods but also to the Holy Spirit, whom I was so familiar with at the convent in Mussoorie! After this, the churning always dissipated. Later, with encouragement from my guru, I exercised total surrender to Ma Kundalini. Once I was able to do that, the rest became an education and an experience that is way beyond the realms of the physical world.

Kundalini as the Creative Energy then took over the task of clearing my physical organism. I now realise that She *is* a Mother to me in what is in effect a new birth, a long, drawn-out process involving the death of the old ego and rebirth into a more expansive consciousness. I would at first relax and watch Her in action; I watched and felt the energy pushing here, nudging there, activating organs that were sluggish, and gently removing blockages. I even sensed Her erasing grooves on the brain cortex and creating new ones. Often, I would wake up from sleep to feel Her weight on a particular spot on my body—sometimes on the belly or on one side of the chest. I would then have to wake up and enter into meditation to allow the energy to naturally disperse all over the body.

I did not resist Her claims on me and went through the whole process of restructuring my essence in a total frame of relaxation, knowing fully well that She would push the mind-body mechanism only within its limits of tolerance. The tenderness and care with which this whole process continued to be handled was beyond words. My suggestion to all aspirants who may be starting on this kind of spiritual awakening under the guidance of a guru is that they should leave themselves without an iota of fear toward the gentle ministrations of Ma Kundalini.

The availability of literature helps when immediate access to the guru is difficult. More often than not, the guru leaves you to find your own answers and draw your own conclusions. At such a stage, any relevant reference material can be of great support to the aspirant undergoing a supramental experience. Sometimes it may also happen that aspirants imagine that they are hallucinating or going crazy, and as a result of feeling scared and out of their wits, it may happen they lose confidence and give up their search. My first-hand account is intended as a reference for aspirants who endeavour to travel on the road to self-discovery. I believe I have put down my experiences on paper so that they may serve as an incentive to other aspirants. It is truly a blessing to know that it is no longer necessary to go to the Himalayas or to become a recluse in order to discover the Self. I was an ordinary person with normal wants and desires, going about my day-to-day work responsibilities and trying to fulfil them to the best of my ability. The exercises not only awakened my hidden and dormant energies but also endowed me with good health, renewed confidence, vigour, and joy, bringing to a conscious level the very nature of my being. I got a better understanding of myself as I started to live my life with a heightened level of awareness. My feeling of well-being also changed during this transformative period. Earlier in my life, I could not define happiness. Instead, I could only think of myself as being contented or discontented. After my experiences began, I could shout at the top of my voice, "I am happy! I am happy! I am happy without any reason! I am just plain happy!"

My daily routine was something like this: I woke up by about four in the morning to immediately sit down for meditation. Before I entered meditation, it was my usual practice to invoke the blessings of my gurus and the enlightened beings, past and present, who have contributed to my spiritual growth, either directly or indirectly through their inspiring books and teachings. At 5:10 a.m., after a cup of weak tea, I would go for a five or six kilometre walk along Marine Drive by the Arabian Sea, where I was often joined by a couple of walking companions who live in the neighbourhood. I worked out a routine of doing my practice of the breaths and affirmations before getting into the daily household duties. By ten, I was ready to leave for office, where I worked on the visuals that had surfaced within my consciousness during the morning meditations. I would try my best to finish the rough drawings to the best of my ability, and add any elements I had missed out on earlier. At one thirty in the afternoon, I would return home for lunch and a brief thirty-minute nap. For at least one hour, from seven to eight every evening, I would engage in serious meditation once again. The rest of my time was spent in attending to responsibilities toward home and family. These activities included reading, sketching, painting, attending special interest classes, shopping, having long chats with family and friends on the phone, and finally going to bed by ten every night.

Attending the weekly lectures became a part of my life, and as the eight-month course finished up, I enrolled in it the next year and continued to do so for the next ten years. Also, as mentioned earlier, Guruji conducted a group meditation once a week, which after his retirement, he shifted to my home.

I religiously tried to record my experiences in meditation, although it was impossible to put down the whole essence. Unless immediately recorded, the visions, the emotions, and the ecstasy would fade away. In any case, no words can infuse the recounting with the varied emotions, the sense of freedom, the total nonbeing, the absence of any ego consciousness that I have experienced. Interestingly, the moon cycle, as it waxed and waned, seemed to strongly affect the pattern of meditation for me. The intensity of meditation lessened around every new moon and was at its height around every full moon, a time now increasingly related to the experience of the Void, where I would lose my identity and be one with it.

The aim of recording my experiences as accurately as possible, as simply as possible, and as completely as possible is that all people going through a similar process of awakening may have a point of reference. The experiences may not be the same, but the essence will perhaps be shared by all. The explanations for the visual experiences are based on my own perceptions. I later came upon the references to these experiences in the texts of various masters, ones which I totally identified with. I think that they accurately explain the visuals as I saw them.

My innate curiosity helped me move at considerable speed in the process of self-discovery. Looking back, I now see that strangely enough for me, meditation has been a very keen, critical, and analytical experience of seeing and understanding in a holistic sense. I was truthfully recording what I saw, felt, and thought, as much as can be conventionally understood of the no-mind state of being. This state is perhaps an example of a spontaneous and effortless manifestation of a multi-pointed focus, or *anekagra dhyan,* which was once pointed out to me by a friend. This stands in contrast to the single-pointed focus, or *ekagra dhyan.*

My portrait taken in 1999 for the back cover of my first book
Conscious Flight Into The Empyrean

THE SUPPORT OF THE GURU

Every single mind-body organism pulsates and vibrates in its own particular individual pattern and has its own particular characteristics. No two psyches are exactly alike; each person will experience inner awakening in his or her own way. Lifetimes of work on the path of spiritual evolution lie nascent at the base of one's essential being, awaiting activation by the guru or master at the appropriate time. Every person is in constant touch with the Inner Source in some way or other. When the time is right, a living guru and the subconsciously seeking *shishya* become part of a spontaneous event of unfolding consciousness, a process signifying an evolutionary leap for the serious disciple.

Confusion, doubts, and mutual testing are perhaps a natural part of this profound relationship between two individuals on the evolutionary path. The more I think about it, I realise that the testing is usually a projection of the disciple's own inner turmoil. On the guru's part, there exists inside him an ever present genuineness, openness, acceptance, and love as the result of being a channel of the Divine. Once the veil of ignorance is lifted from the student's mind, there comes an almost instantaneous recognition of the divinity of the guru, bringing in its wake a surge of gratitude and surrender to the master. In this transformative moment lies the seed of the transmutation of several lifetimes of karma, which brings to fruition the manifestation of Grace in the life of the seeker.

It is my impression that women are all too often discouraged from seeking direct spiritual guidance on the yogic path, especially if the guru happens to be a man.

While it is true that there are always dangers of going astray given the strong nature of the bond in the guru-shishya relationship, the level of maturity of true seekers on the path must override such dangers. The experience of love for one's guru and the opportunity to freely and openly express this emotion without lowering the connection's higher vibrations to the level of mundane corruption is in fact what brings in the operation of Grace for the disciple. There is no doubt in my mind that it was my guru's genuine concern for my well-being that guided my onward journey, mundane as well as spiritual, from moment to moment and protected me from the strong buffeting winds of destiny.

My guru had more or less maintained a stoic silence throughout, playing the role of a patient listener and of a silent guide. It is unfathomable to me as to how he could generate within me a perception of encouragement, admonishment, and gentleness without voicing any opinion. Paradoxically, he seemed to take care of everything without seeming to take care of anything. He had always been by my side, guiding me by word as well as by silence, with the utmost care, gentleness, and firmness.

The guru not only serves as a mascot for the outward projection of the inner teacher but is also a very nurturing, accepting, and reassuring presence when at times the process of awakening brings distress. I think I was brought to my guru at the most opportune moment in my life so that he could subtly initiate the process of guiding me as I ventured further on the path of spiritual evolution. A cleansing of my mind and body had ensued thereafter and perhaps still continues to this day.

I visualised the guru as the Ultimate Reality, the living principle through which one may experience God. The knowledge most important to my psyche was that the Highest Reality had manifested Itself as human in the form of my guru. This concept was depicted in a vision as my guru sitting on the Cosmic Wheel, which is the symbol of the Universal Law. Going over the visuals several months later, I was so deeply moved by this vision that it resulted thereafter in a total surrender on my part to the guru and his teachings.

Having lived through this profound experience of growing inner awareness, I can now appreciate the teachings of Brahma Vidya in the fullest sense. I understand that faithfully following the principles of this teaching leads to self-mastery and the realisation of our highest capabilities. It has been the greatest honour and privilege for me to be chosen as a disciple on this unique visual voyage of the greatest teachings accessible to human beings—the secret of existence. Being brought to the awareness that the riddle of the Universe is about me and that I am solving it has been a very humbling experience.

I must mention here that whatever words the guru uttered, I would automatically adhere to. This was not only true for simple words and phrases such as "relax" and "watch your breath." It was also true for instructions to stand in the open first thing in the morning and "open out your arms, asking the Void to unfold your purpose" or to send forth love into the world. I began to realise the power of these words nearly two years after hearing them constantly from the mouth of the guru. Among the most potent words were, "Watch your breath. See where it touches."

I realised that the breath that I took for granted is actually the vehicle that circulates prana, the life force, through the body. When we follow any chosen breathing technique, we can experience subtler dimensions of consciousness. It is the breath that paves the way for Kundalini, so that She can do Her work without any impediment. When the guru instructed me to watch where the breath touches, it became most fascinating to watch because it followed a certain pattern. It touched one particular point for a couple of breaths. When the work there was done, the focus shifted to another point, all the while moving through the left nostril. That is, the breath came in straight from the nostril, but I felt it move at different angles in different parts of the body. It was not as if it was moving through an intricately constructed territory but through a smooth plain surface. Just as one surrenders to the guru and to Kundalini, so also should one surrender to the breath, for then only can the course of spiritual evolution become not one of resistance but one of faith in the innate goodness of the universe.

As I was undergoing this curious adventure, what seemed to come in the way was my questioning nature about the why, when, how, and where of things. Guruji told me that the intellect must transcend the realm of body and mind because the Infinite cannot be known by the finite. If I kept on with the whys and the hows, I would miss out on the Omnipresent Reality. I had to bring myself to that level of knowing that was appropriate to that which was to be known.

I suppose my earlier reactions were quite natural. I was totally unprepared for the phenomena I experienced, not realising that I was being given a lesson in the process of creation itself. This lesson instructed me about how the body is composed of the same subtle elements—earth, air, water, fire, and ether—as the atmosphere we live and breathe in. The fact was brought home to me that I was more than this physical body, which is only an abode of "the transcendentally beautiful, the infinitely intricate, and the most gloriously accurate instrument in the Universe," as it is said in one of the affirmations. I realised the body was for my use for many lifetimes as a vehicle to work my way up from the grossest to the subtlest way of being.

Thus far in meditation, I had been given just cursory knowledge and experiences of clairvoyance, clairaudience, astral travel, and fragrances. I had not been allowed to dwell too much upon these phenomena. People told me about the special *siddhis*, or supernatural powers, that follow the awakening of the kundalini. I had experienced many of these in an altered state of consciousness in the course of my meditations, including, for example, astral travel. The course had taken me into realms that are only to be experienced. Otherwise, I was simply operating as a normal person going about my daily duties. As I used to tell myself, I had been led away from the by-lanes of siddhis that might have distracted me from the goal.

It is not possible for me to bring forth on paper all the encounters, thoughts, feelings, sounds, fragrances and sights experienced by me in that state of consciousness. Words cannot describe the wonder, joy, beauty, rapture, and radiance that pervade those dimensions; I think it is futile to even make the attempt. Meanwhile, I had a lot to learn from my guru. If, for some reason, I were to be chosen to be the instrument of this glorious unfoldment, I knew its purpose would be fulfilled, and the events would take their own course. I was only a willing participant.

From the very beginning, there was within me a subliminal awareness that my journal would one day become a book. While the purpose of such a book was not at all clear to me at that time, I did try to maintain as complete a record as possible. On the other hand, in order to develop a fair balance in all my areas of functioning, I had to maintain a rather rigid compartmentalisation of each separate area of my life, particularly the meditation sessions. I was convinced that the visuals were not related to my personal state of being. As I see it, they did not primarily emerge out of my personal unconscious but were the externally manipulated, step-by-step revelations of a yogic reality as it manifested in my life during the meditations and the affirmations.

I was aware that my body-mind configuration was continually subjected to subtle adjustment from an external agency, the source of which I am as of yet completely unaware. I had consciously, unquestioningly, and effortlessly surrendered to this force from day one. There were distinct phases of meditational experience brought on as the direct result of these changes. These included seeing the prana, seeing the chakras, becoming aware of the shifts in vibration, astral travel, glimpses of past lives, and entering the Void. This Void, as I experienced it, is a place where it is neither day nor night, neither dusk nor dawn. It is nothing—it only *is.* One can only experience it. Trying to put it into words is meaningless. There were times when the nudges and shoves were physically palpable. I had become increasingly aware of changes wrought in the functioning of the internal organs, and especially of the brain. I was sometimes aware of a feeling that the brain was actually moving to the left or right in the cranium as I shifted from analytical thinking to the more intuitive or dream-like state. As mentioned earlier, one of my vivid memories is of the kundalini energy mechanically erasing the grooves on my brain and creating new ones!

On several occasions, I experienced travelling long distances through tunnels, sometimes under a starry sky. I have conjectured that this type of internal journey might in fact be nothing more than going through special channels inside the brain itself. Many times, at the end of such a journey, I found myself in the

Hall of Akashic Records. The hall seemed to have huge golden gates, a floor with big squares, and a wall of bright light. As I progressed in meditation toward meeting and merging with Source Consciousness, I wondered if such voyages involve a life and death experience for the subtle body, a process that might erase lifetimes of good or bad karma.

The present earthly time does not operate during these voyages in meditation. Within every preset period of meditation, I was always aware of having achieved an incredible amount of observing and experiencing. This process also included communicating with other beings, travelling to other realms, and learning from them.

While engaged in meditation, I was seldom disturbed by external influences, sounds, wayward thoughts, or people moving about in the room. I was rarely upset, agitated, or frightened by the strange goings-on that the visions portrayed, and I remained fully conscious and aware at all such times. I found myself making invocations to the guru or fervently chanting a mantra like *Om Shanti* if, for example, there was a vision of a herd of massive wild elephants charging full speed at me or if my body was shaken by an out-of-control surge of the kundalini energy in the *muladhara chakra*. With experience, I knew that the force would subside and take a more benign form. My faith had never been belied. I never flinched when I saw surgical implements like drills and needles advance toward me or when I was shown the insides of my head being scraped, as if it were on a fully lit screen of a monitor. I had fully cooperated with the unseen agency and clearly stated my willingness to learn what was being taught at each different stage in this deeply spiritual adventure.

It is true that the lectures, exercises, affirmations, and meditations were totally unrelated to my daily life. They were apart from other essential areas of my life as a mother, householder, and businesswoman. At the same time, the techniques had changed me from inside out to such an extent that I found myself a different person from whom I was previously. I became a much more positive, happy, and youthful person than I ever was before. To be honest, I felt that I had recovered the essence of a lively, joyous, and carefree way of being that had existed for me during my youth in Mussoorie. The intervening years, between the passing away of Ajeet and my spiritual unfoldment, had brought a fair share of responsibilities and conformity to social expectations, particularly as a dutiful wife and mother. What happened after engaging in meditation was that several layers of my conditioned identity had been progressively peeled off to reveal an underlying core of natural radiance, fluidity, poise, grace, and love in my life.

BEING LIVED

The lessons, exercises, and affirmations had started in me a process of conscious living and evolving. All creation has a certain pattern to it and moves within its orbit with an unwavering precision. The truth has dawned that all creation, animate and inanimate, follows a certain fixed and rhythmic pattern of evolution and dissolution. If I, as a thinking and conscious entity, will only allow myself to flow with the scheme of things ordained for me, I will complete my cycle in a peaceful and harmonious manner without blocking the process that Nature has planned for me. This way of existing is not difficult for me. Somehow, I have always felt intuitively that I am not living my life but that rather life is being lived through me. I do not go out to meet life; rather it comes to meet me. I am just there for it. The practice of Brahma Vidya has given this clarity to my being.

Since I had been given the ability to see my thought forms, I have discovered that every single thought has a corresponding form that travels at a very fast speed, attracting good or bad, love or hate. It follows the dictum by Jesus, "As you sow, so shall you reap." The thoughts that we send out into the Universal Consciousness act like a magnet and therefore attract similar thoughts from all directions.

This experience has made me wiser and helped me realise the ultimate purpose of life. The individual consciousness, created with certain specific characteristics, is set loose in a maze at the start of its manifestation and is expected to find its way back to the Source. In the process, it gets caught up in a web of thoughts, actions, deeds, and emotions. It thus loses its identity, focus, and purpose for lives upon lives until one fine day it starts questioning the hows, whens, and whys of existence. What is life all about? Once these queries begin, it starts to unravel the confusion that has been created and then spends further lives working its way back to the Source.

I became a serious student in order to know and learn what was transpiring. For this, not only my body and its *koshas* had to go through a purification process; the mind also had to be tuned to work to perfection. In order for this to happen, meditation was a must.

GROUP MEDITATION STARTS AT HOME

In 1997, Guruji retired after completing his long tenure of dispensing justice in the Bombay High Court. In due course, he had to vacate the government accommodation allotted to him. Since we could not meet for meditation at his residence, I suggested that we could meet at my apartment. This suited everyone, as our flat is centrally located.

That day, when it came, was a big day for me and my children. With his presence in my home came a great deal of joy and an activity that I would enthusiastically look forward to. Every Tuesday, the hall would be cleared of furniture for the group meditation.

The first Tuesday was a bit confusing for me as I did not have the faintest idea of how I should receive him when he came. Normally, when the guru comes to a devotee's home, it is a festive, though formal, occasion. However, my guru was not conventional. At his residence, we had held a general get-together before settling down for meditation. I was all excited on that Tuesday, waiting for the time when he would arrive. The aspirants started coming in by six in the evening and settling down. A little later, Guruji came, and the only way I could receive him was with a big hug and the words, "We are blessed." In my excitement, I forgot to offer him anything to drink or eat. When I asked Guruji in which direction he would like to sit, he said he was fine with whatever was convenient.

The rest of the meditation took place more or less the same way it did at his residence.

Next week, however, I was more settled and asked him if he would like a cup of tea or some fruits. He replied, "Serve everyone tea." Thus every Tuesday, it became a ritual before sitting for meditation to have some tea and snacks. Guruji would come and sit at the dining table, and a few eager people would occupy the chairs around the table, while others would sit a bit away on the sofa, chairs, or carpet. It became a relaxed, enjoyable evening with Guruji; his energy lifted everyone's spirits before we would sit for meditation.

I was very happy serving the snacks and picking up empty cups and plates at the end of it. Nothing went unnoticed by Guruji. One evening, when it was time for meditation, he looked around at everyone and saw I was still busy clearing plates. Seeing that I was overworked a bit, he addressed the group and asked them if they would get up and help. After that, the clearing happened much more quickly, with plenty of time for me to relax and settle down for meditation.

The weekly routine was set. I would put a *toran* at the door of my apartment every Tuesday. During festivals, the passage and the hall would be decorated with flowers, and incense sticks would spread fragrance all around.

My friends would ask me how I was managing to do all that I was doing. Balancing Brahma Vidya, home life, and my work did not really seem a problem. I never thought about it, and life had fallen into a pattern. I was able to look after the home, children, office, and attend lectures once a week. In addition to this, I recorded my experiences, setting them into words, and I also hosted group meditations in my home. I realised that I had time for everything. I tried to observe myself and came to an understanding that this whole routine was meant to be. So nature, the higher forces, or destiny had my life's pattern all planned out meticulously.

I was able to do all this happily because of the support system I had been provided by my brother, Shiv, by my children and staff at my home and office, and by my guru, who came and placed himself in my home.

With Justice Dudhat at my residence before the group meditation

SHIFTS

As one grows from childhood to adulthood, a natural and gradual shift, which one is totally unware of, takes place in one's consciousness. It is a smooth transition from one level to the other. The brain structure and grooves in it develop accordingly. It is a constant development that goes on as adjustment to one's life situations occur.

However, if one is following a programme in self-development, the process is different, particularly if one is following Kundalini Yoga. The only way for an aspirant to go through this yoga is to have full faith in the guru and a complete surrender to the energy the path awakens. The aspirant must also possess the knowledge that whatever his or her mind, body, and intellect goes through during sadhana is only for his or her own good.

As I followed the path of Kundalini Yoga, I realised that my salvation lay in surrendering to the energy and fearlessly leaving myself open to its working. The clearing of my mental, emotional, and physical blocks was hastened by the awakened kundalini, which meant that the solidified blocks had to be chiseled and dissolved for the energy to make any headway. This naturally caused pain and discomfort, shoves and nudges, and jerks and twinges, because the energy that is moving is all-powerful and will not have any obstacles in its path.

The meridians in the subtle body are not expanded enough to take on the extra load and hence go into a spasm when the energy moves, which is reflected in the physical body as jerks. In addition to pain, soundless popping and shattering astral sounds accompanied the regulating and adjusting of my chakras, which seemed to have gotten stuck due to lack of harmony in my body-mind intellect. I feel I am one of the lucky ones, for I quite enjoyed the experience. One can imagine the immensity of the power that lies dormant within us at the base of the spine when one realises that it is the same energy that causes an earthquake when it moves under the surface of the earth.

It was more of an adventure, probably because it was a journey into the unknown, a journey that had no milestones or warning signs. The child in me was most curious to follow the visual experience through, taking in stride whatever obstacles came along and seeing where this all was leading. I became apprehensive when the work on the brain started, for this was no child's play. It was serious business. Could I leave my psyche open to any short circuits that might take place? Could I risk going mad? These were the few questions that came to my mind. Could I risk my sanity for the thrill of adventure and excitement? After much thought, I resumed my practice, safe and secure in the knowledge that if so far I had been treated with gentleness, love, and understanding, there was no reason for it to be otherwise at this crucial juncture.

After consideration and reviewing my faith in myself, I was once again acted upon by the gentle force of Kundalini, who now started Her work minutely and efficiently, like a master craftsman. In order to make it easy for me, I was given a full understanding of what was being done in my brain. For me, the shifts that would probably take lifetimes were being cut short by the transference of the meaning of the affirmations, which were then memorised by the left brain and interpreted by the right brain. This ultimately gave me the ability to understand the deep meaning that was being conveyed by the visual unfoldment.

Certain parts in the brain had to be stretched by inserting a sharp instrument into the tissue or membrane. Then the grooves of the frontal lobe had to be erased and reinscribed. The whole exercise is quite painful and can take days, depending on the individual's level of tolerance.

I had to go through the process of transformation in order to fulfil the desire to know my Source. I realise how important it is to be conscious and aware of each thought we have or express because, in doing so, we set the whole body structure in motion to produce the result.

So it is: we should be cautious about expressing thoughts, wishes, and desires at random because we have no idea of what we are doing to ourselves!

The meditations became significantly different. Perhaps I was moving toward further unfoldment. I felt a finger place itself on my forehead between the eyebrows (ajna chakra) and applying pressure till I stopped all the affirmations.

I felt the subtle head within my head turning like a revolving door. The adjustment was somewhat stressful. I also found the body within trying to move in the same manner.

The chakra at the back of the head started to get active, bringing about a smoother functioning of the whole process. I saw a man's face talking to me. It seemed like a face from another planet; the features were like ours, but the shape of the face was slightly different. The main difference was in the ears and the jaw. The jaw had a problem forming the words. Was I supposed to learn something? I don't know if I did! My head was still slightly heavy. The process was probably to prepare my subtle body for the next step.

What I then saw is reproduced on the following page, as it appeared in my third book, *Kundalini Awakening.*

December 7, 1998

A beam of white light starts from a point at the back of the head, near about where the neck and head meet. It projects itself out, curves over the head like a big cobra hood and, still curving over the front of the body, enters the chest. Simultaneously, another beam of light projects from the same point and shoots up like an antenna into the cosmos.

This point at the base of the head (which was activated with acupuncture earlier) would now serve for me as the connecting point or as the service station between the individual consciousness and Source Consciousness. It is awe inspiring to know that I am now directly connected with the Source. Wow!!!

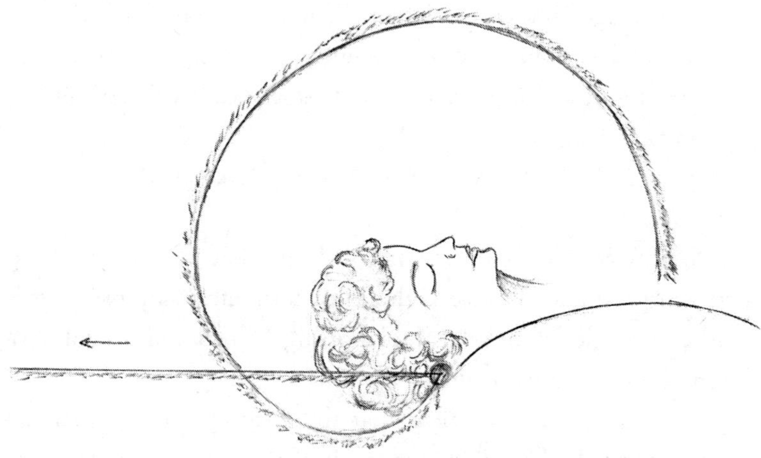

The diary entry (left) supported by the drawing as it appeared in my third book, *Kundalini Awakening*, 200–201

SYMBOLS

'In India, ajna chakra is called *divya chakshu* ("the divine eye"), *jnana chakshu*, or *jnana netra* ("the eye of knowledge") because it is the channel through which the spiritual aspirant receives revelation and insight into the underlying nature of existence. It is also called the eye of Shiva.'

—Swami Satyananda Saraswati, *Kundalini Tantra*

Swami Satyananda Saraswati tells us that "the relationship between guru and disciple is the most intimate relationship; it is neither a religious nor a legal relationship. Guru and disciple live like an object and its shadow."

What I noticed as well is that the guru's grace is constantly flowing toward all of us. How many of us awaken and get onto the bandwagon of sadhana depends entirely on our receptivity, willingness to trust, ability to surrender, and level of evolution.

A meaningful experience I had in meditation that illustrates this point occurred when my siblings and I, as children, were once standing in front of a pandit. Turn by turn, we bent forward so that he could put a tikka on our foreheads. When I leaned forward, he drew with his thumb a *yantra* in the form of a square spiral onto my forehead.

Later, I received the insight that this yantra was the symbol

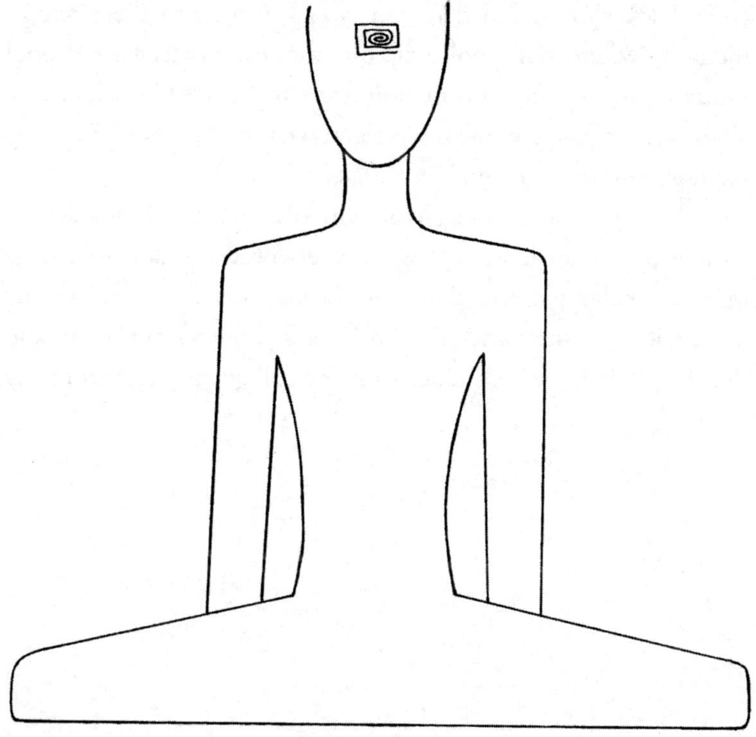

The drawing as it appeared in my third book *Kundalini Awakening*, 225

of a labyrinth, a design which relates to wholeness. That is, the labyrinth represents a journey to our own centre and then from there out into the external world.

My understanding of the two symbols I experienced in meditation, a drop of water and the spiral, was that when my awareness moved as a spiral, I would go right into the centre and come back with stored data as it was getting into the recess of memory. Whereas, if I took a dip into the cosmic ocean as a drop, I found I was accessing information from the Source Consciousness. These symbols helped me understand what had surfaced from my memory and from the higher realms.

It is my understanding that symbols considered sacred were created by the ancient sages who experienced the flow of energy in a particular pattern. Some of the insights I received in my meditations on the forms of Lord Ganesha, the Shiva trident, and the temple bell are reproduced on the following pages from my diary.

A u g u s t 2 3, 1 9 9 7

The ajna chakra elongates and moves within the body. It moves in different directions, surveying its deepest regions. The extended and elongated chakra looked like an elephant's trunk, and it gave me an insight as to how Ganpati got his form. This meditation further activated my ajna chakra, the source of all knowledge.

The drawing as it appeared in my third book *Kundalini Awakening*, 118–119

February 23, 2000

There is a meeting of descending and ascending energy. There is no feeling of a body from the chest upward. There is no neck and head. Instead the entire area of the abdomen and above is only light, and what is visible is a good-sized pendulum moving like a temple bell beyond the sahasrara chakra (crown chakra). Fascinating! The individual consciousness remains as a shining flame ready to merge with the consciousness at rest, the Source.

Going through the above experience and contemplating and meditating on it has cleared the process of my thought completely. I recall Guruji's words each time I would ask him to explain the meaning of my experience. His response was often, "Wait. It will unfold in time."

I realise that once the dense body starts to become subtle, once the denseness starts to fall off, what remains is a drop, the individual consciousness, which is ready to fall into the ocean of Source Consciousness. Till such a time happens, it will continue to be a pendulum and toll as a resounding bell, as if from a church steeple or a temple, and be the wake-up call for those ready to know themselves and move on to the road of self-discovery, leading out of the cycle of birth and death. That is, the process going from subtle consciousness to dense consciousness and from dense consciousness to subtle, and so on.

I marvel every time I get an insight into the astuteness of our *rishis.* They created a symbol for everything they experienced at the subtle level. The human body is given the symbol of a temple and a church, with the bell symbolising the Source residing within us. Just as we go into a temple and we see and worship the deity, if we were to go within ourselves, we would come face to face with that part of the Source that is residing within us as individual consciousness.

The diary entry (left) supported by the drawing as it appeared in my third book, *Kundalini Awakening*, 238–239

February 23, 2000

The centre point of the *trishul*, the symbol of the Shaivites, also represents Consciousness, with the rod symbolising the shining sushumna. The trishul is always carried by them or placed next to wherever they are sitting; it automatically raises the consciousness to the crown chakra and above.

I give below a few lines from the affirmation that goes with my experience of the visual:

> My body—the temple, the temple of the Living God, the temple of the God who lives within me—that is alive within me. I stand in reverence before the wisdom pent up in the very substance of my body, and I pledge myself, I vow, that from this moment henceforth nothing that I shall do, say, or think shall injure or abuse this temple of the Living God, my body.

The book of my unfoldment makes me wonder at the process of my experience. I am sure the knowledge that is channeled through me has a purpose. I offer my humble thanks and gratitude to my guru, to the masters, and to the Higher Forces for finding this body-mind intellect worthy of their purpose.

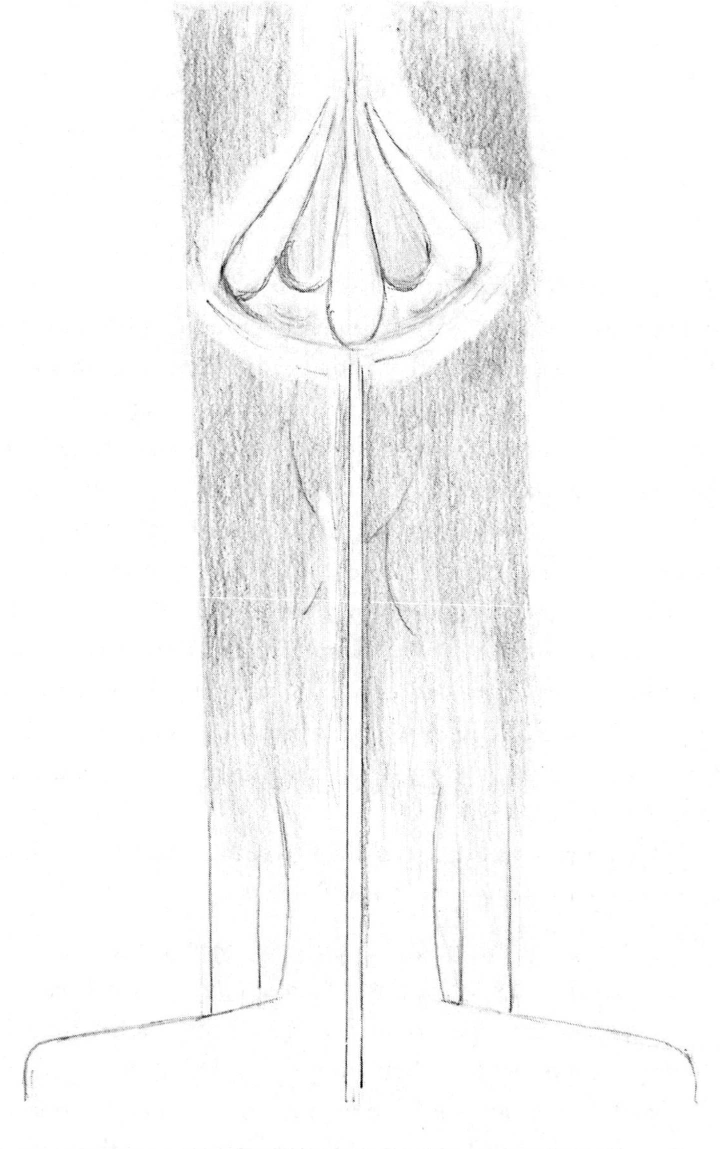

The drawing as it appeared in my third book, *Kundalini Awakening*, 240–241

DEATH AND AFTER

Sitting down for meditation in the early hours of the morning on February 24, 2004, I saw a beam of light extend from the ajna chakra and trace a path up the forehead, a process enabling my consciousness to move out from the centre at the top of the head. Piercing the cosmos, the light created a ripple and merged with the Source Consciousness. Simultaneously, all the chakras in the different parts of the body started unwinding, expanding, and merging with the different elements they are composed of. What was left moving was a subtle form resembling the yin-yang symbol at the manipura chakra level. I suspected this form was probably a bundle of unresolved desires waiting to attach itself to another fragmented part of consciousness, which then moves toward the denser dimensions of existence to exhaust its karmas and move toward wholeness.

This process was described by Osho in his book *Zen Tarot: The Transcendental Game of Zen* as follows:

> The image of integration is the *unio mystica*, the fusion of opposites. This is a time of communication between the previously experienced dualities of life. Rather than night opposing day, dark suppressing light, they work together to create a unified whole, turning endlessly one into the other, each containing in its deepest core the seed of the opposite.

The drawing as it appeared in my third book, *Kundalini Awakening*, 243

It took me about twelve years to solve the riddle of the Universe that was about me. During this time, I went through the process of learning and understanding the intricate pattern that has been set for the evolution of human consciousness. The time had now come for me to consciously go through the process of the body's death and ultimate expansion.

A time came when the role of the guru principle was complete in my current life, and I was left to integrate the knowledge that had been accumulated.

During meditation, I saw in the deep blue void the form of the guru. The form was bathed in light; the head was also radiating rays of light. Slowly and steadily, the form started sinking into the void and then disappeared. I assumed that the journey of unfoldment—which had started for me on November 1, 1995, with the manifestation of the guru—was now complete, and the guru principle deemed it appropriate to leave me on my own to move on at my own pace.

This knowledge, this experience, and this creativity is possible when the guru-disciple relationship manifests at the deepest level of existence and transcends duality and when one can remain receptive to the impulses flowing from the Divine from within and without.

Would the Source reveal Itself so completely to an individual? Why? Is it in preparation for the times that are to come? Are we moving toward a time where we are going to have a different understanding? Does it mean that henceforth our evolution will start with the awareness of Source Consciousness? Will I get an answer to my questions? Yes. I already see young aspirants who are awakening and moving toward a new understanding of what we worship as God.

MASTER CHARLES CANNON

Going down memory lane, a past incident came to my mind of my father tapping the outer part of my feet with his walking stick when I was walking ahead of him. This was done to make sure that I would walk with my feet straight instead of with them facing outward.

I feel life similarly kept nudging me gently to remain on the path that I had been formally initiated into by our family guru. This process was also carried on by my continued contact with spiritual masters, who kept me moving on the path until I fulfilled the purpose for which I was destined.

My daughter Nikki had met Master Charles Cannon in Hong Kong in the latter part of 1997 and remained under his spiritual guidance for a number of years. Master Charles is a spiritual teacher and founder of the Synchronicity Foundation, based in Virginia. While the teaching was being imparted to me through the lectures of Brahma Vidya, I was simultaneously receiving insights through Master Charles' newsletters and recorded videos. The newsletters gave me the essence of teachings that led to clarity of thought and understanding of my experiences.

My guru once said, "A thought arose in Consciousness to see Itself in multitude, and Creation happened." I discovered an in-depth understanding of this statement in one of Master Charles' newsletters:

> As the Source Consciousness fragmented in multidimensional experience from subtle to dense, holistic awareness is forfeited. The field of relative oscillation accelerates, and the polarities seem to be separate from each other. Thus, the truth is being Source, and the illusion is not being Source. This is fragmented experience.
>
> As One Source Consciousness densifies, the negative polarity dominates the positive polarity…or illusion dominates the truth; thus, the separation is illusory duality. Illusion, however, is always pretence that becoming is different and separate from being, the object is different and separate from subject. This is the Creation Game. As Source, I create an illusion…a form of Myself that I do not recognise so that I may experience recognition and magnify my experience, my bliss, in the process. This is the cosmic game, and as with all games, it is played for the fun of it.

Guruji would say, "Be a witness to whatever arises in the moment." I had never understood how to be a witness to what arises in the moment until it happened. In the same way, the witnessing of my breath's movements also happened to me and was not something I apprehended with my intellect. I realised that "doing" does not work. If I could just be, new dimensions, I realised, would open up, while witnessing would become more like watching a movie on a cinema screen. The question was how this process would happen. I found it clearly answered in one of the newsletters:

> When the primary trinity of the physical, emotional, and mental dimensions are in balance, the subtle dimension opens up as witness consciousness, as a detached observer

> of the relative field. Herein, we are watching the physical, emotional, and mental dimensions from the now dominant subtle dimension of witness consciousness. Yet, the mental dimension has several levels, and complete detachment from them is a gradual process in meditation.
>
> Firstly, there is gross level of data and interpretation. Then, there are more subtle levels of mental impressions with less interpretation and data processing. As the witness consciousness in the subtle dimension becomes more dominant and constant in meditation, there is complete detachment from all the levels of the mental dimension. Then, there is just the observation of stillness. Remember we meditate to be present, to simply watch the experience that is happening. By simply watching, we simply extract our focus from the physical, mental, and emotional dimensions, and they progressively become still. Then, we are watching stillness, and then we progress to a more subtle state of pure awareness in the causal and supra-causal dimensions.

Finally, Master Charles clarifies the guru-disciple relationship. He writes, "So the question of how Conscious Living is experienced as a practical reality can only be answered in the light of the disciple's intention. Masters themselves are neither easy nor difficult. They simply serve as a pure reflection of what each individual creates in relation to them. Everything hinges on the disciple."

Going through the newsletters on a daily basis added clarity to the nondual and dual aspects of reality. The nondual can only be understood through manifestation. In other words, Consciousness as a whole does not know Itself. In order to know Itself, It has to manifest as another.

In due course, when the time came to publish the journal of my experiences, I went to seek permission from my guru and other gurus but did not get a clear answer from them. On the contrary, I was asked a counterquestion as to why I wanted to publish the book. "It was my experience," I answered usually. "It would help other aspirants who were going through their experience." Still I did not get a clear go-ahead, and I wondered why.

I wrote to Master Charles. He gave a very clear answer through a letter explaining the reason for the masters not giving their assent easily.

> Santosh…of the One,
>
> I remain delighted when I consider the part you play in our world.
>
> Thank you for sharing your book with me. It is most appropriate and will undoubtedly be of assistance to many seekers of truth. I trust that your meditative journey will continue to unfold through ever greater expansions in Sourceful awareness.
>
> In your letter to me that accompanied the book, you mentioned that many masters had questioned why you wrote the book and that this puzzled you. In the tradition of enlightening masters, it is said that one should not reveal their experiences until they receive the command of their master to do so. These masters are just calling your attention to this protocol to ensure that you are clear within yourself that the sharing of your experience must be from the highest dimensions of your Sourceful self and not merely from any egotistical expression. It seems to me that your intention is Sourceful, and therefore your

book has come into manifestation as a direct result. This is indeed appropriate. Therefore, I am sure that it will assist many and that your ongoing journey of ever enlightening awareness will continue.

Once again, I thank you for sharing the book with me, and I look forward to one day meeting you in person.

I hold you in my Sourceful awareness with love.

—Master Charles

After the sanction from Master Charles, the journal went into publication in November 1999 and was released in February 2000.

It was in the beginning of 2008 that Alan Scherr, vice president of Synchronicity Foundation, came to Mumbai to identify the location and hotel for Master Charles and his group of about twenty-five members, who were planning a visit to Mumbai in November. My children Nikki and Gautam had arranged a programme for his discourses and meditations at an auditorium in South Mumbai. The venue for his stay was chosen after much deliberation. It was to be The Oberoi Hotel at Nariman Point.

During the week or so that Alan was in Mumbai, he would send regular updates through e-mail on his visit to subscribers of the Synchronicity newsletter. He sent me a copy of one of the newsletters, which was deeply touching and which said the following:

Dear Friends,

I am blessed to know someone here in India who truthfully identifies herself as Source. She is the mother of the family with whom Master Charles and Synchronicity have partnered with in our recent trips to India. Her son is the founder of one of India's leading spiritual publishing houses, and her daughter is a long-term Recognitions Associate who has maintained a close connection with Master Charles over many years.

Mataji, or dear mother, as we call her, is one of those rare individuals who has experienced an advanced awakening of kundalini through many stages of unfoldment in the context of a classical guru-disciple relationship. Along the way, she has had profound visionary experiences that represent, in symbolic and archetypal terms, the many and varied transformations and phenomena that accompany this awakening of the Divine within, as Master Charles has termed it.

Out of her experience, she has created a series of books that include simple but profoundly powerful drawings that serve to give expression to the unfolding of her unique spiritual journey, particularly the awakening of kundalini. The focus of Mataji's writings is the guru-disciple relationship, which she places at the core of authentic spiritual awakening. In the spirit of modern mysticism, she has also enthusiastically adopted Master Charles' Holistic Model of Reality, which she says has allowed her to more precisely articulate the subtle dimensional realities that had previously been challenging to express.

To be with Mataji is to experience the joyful presence of a human being whose awareness is focused in the now. She has lived a full life, having raised three children, each of whom has subsequently embraced the spiritual journey, while herself simultaneously running a successful business. For a number of years, her focus has been her writing as well as serving as a spiritual teacher to a number of her students with whom she meets on a regular basis to guide them in their meditative practice.

As Master Charles says, "In the great Play of Consciousness, everyone appropriately plays their role."

When Master Charles and his group visited Mumbai in November, Gautam invited them for dinner on our building terrace. It was a beautiful evening, and we got to interact closely with them. Gautam had invited some of his friends as well.

With Master Charles Cannon at my residence

On the next evening, after the group meditation at the auditorium, everyone went back to the hotel knowing little of the drama that was to unfold shortly in the form of the terrorist attack on Mumbai. Alan and his beloved thirteen-year-old daughter, Naomi, were shot dead in the restaurant of The Oberoi, while other members of the group had a miraculous escape. It was a dark night for the city, one in which many lives were lost across multiple locations, especially in South Mumbai. It was ironic that during his earlier visit, Alan had mentioned in the course of conversation that he would like to die in India.

Master Charles' visit marked another chapter in my life in the form of an acknowledgement of my spiritual evolution. In addition to the talks, there were silent group meditations organised for those who wished to attend them in the evenings. For these meditations, he asked for a chair to be placed for me next to his seat. I was overwhelmed at the honour he bestowed upon me. At the end of the meditation, the congregation would come to bow to him and then to me. Once this was over, he would ask me to leave the hall with him. Thus, a pattern was set: I would meet him in the room allotted for his rest, and then we would walk in for the meditation together and leave together.

Master Charles helped me to acknowledge myself, and he opened my mind up to what would unfold in terms of being comfortable in the role of guide and guru.

In Master Charles, I found a master who, without any reservations, would empower an aspirant by acknowledging her experience and journey. This acknowledgement gave the energy within me the freedom to flow forth freely—without any doubt, fear, or blocks—so that the energy could initiate aspirants who came within its ambit. Was this acceptance coming from the knowledge that Master Charles had received when he travelled the same road, in all its twists and turns, with his Guru Swami Muktananda of Ganeshpuri? He was one of Muktananda's closest disciples and was given the title Swami Vivekananda Saraswati by his master.

As I look back with awareness on my meeting with different spiritual masters, I realise the love that unconditionally flows from them. Only if we are nonjudgmental do we recognise it.

With Alan Scherr on our building terrace

ECKHART TOLLE

In early 1999, my friend Meena and I decided to visit my daughter Nikki who was then working in Hong Kong. Nikki's friends had come across a new book, *The Power of Now*. They were so taken up by the subject that they decided to visit its author, Eckhart Tolle, in Vancouver. During their visit, they established a warm bond with Eckhart and invited him to visit Hong Kong. It so happened that my visit to Hong Kong in 2000 coincided with that of Eckhart's. This came as a blessing as we had the opportunity

Nikki and I with Eckhart Tolle at Lantau Island in Hong Kong

to be in the energy field of an enlightened master. There were meditations in the evening. He also visited us at Nikki's apartment. The beautiful thing about being with Eckhart was the transmission that occurred through his eyes. One's eyes would naturally and gradually lock into his gaze when you were around him. The feeling I would get from him was that he was looking through and beyond my eyes and more deeply into something that was not on the physical plane. That moment would seem endless.

After this initial encounter, we spent quite a bit of time with Eckhart. We would do lunches and go sightseeing together, and we seemed like one big family, with everyone absorbed in his energetic presence. During this time, Meena and I had an opportunity to attend his retreat in beautiful surroundings at a hotel in Lantau.

One evening, while a few of us were spending some time in Eckhart's company, we decided to sit for meditation. We all settled down and closed our eyes to meditate. After some time, a mobile

Eckhart Tolle with Justice M. L. Dudhat at my residence

phone rang and startled everyone out of the meditation. Someone got up and turned off the ringtone. The phone rang three times consecutively till finally the lady switched it off. What I found remarkable about this incident was that not a frown appeared on Eckhart's face, nor did his gentle demeanour change. In fact, he added with a sense of humour that this meditation would be remembered as "the meditation when the phone rang thrice," or something to that effect.

In February 2002, Gautam and Nikki invited Eckhart to Mumbai. He gave discourses over two days in South Mumbai. We invited him home for dinner after the talk, and I also took this opportunity to make my guru and Eckhart meet at our home.

DIARY TO MANUSCRIPT TO BOOK LAUNCH

Sri Ma Amodini Saraswati

It was in 1996 or 1997 that I became part of a small group that would meet once a week to discuss subjects of mutual interest. We would talk about belief systems, mantras, energy work, past-life regression, and so on. There was a fiery zeal in me to put my experiences down in the form of a book, but I did not know how to go about it. I talked about it with my friends Rohini and Kaity and invited them to come over to my place to see what I had written. By then, I had put together some sort of a manuscript that consisted of my illustrations and diary notes.

Kaity and Rohini came over, accompanied by another lady named Anjali, whom I hadn't met before and who, they informed me, had a PhD in social welfare from the University of California, Berkeley. I gave them copies of the manuscript, and over a cup of tea, we discussed what could be done with it. It was decided that they would take the manuscript home and think about it, and we would meet me again in a week's time. Anjali asked if she could also have one copy, as she would like to read through it, too.

The three of them came over after a week. I was fascinated to see that Anjali had created a detailed synopsis of the whole experience. As we spoke, the impression I got from her was that this was some sort of rare revelation and had to be treated with a high degree of seriousness with due respect. My son, Gautam, advised that if Anjali could help edit the manuscript, then perhaps something more tangible could take shape, which would develop into a book.

Anjali agreed to this proposal, and full credit goes to her for working very hard with me day and night to draw out the essence and authenticity of this experience. She felt that I had not yet realised the depth and magnitude of all that had been revealed to me by the higher forces. She did not take me at my word. She painstakingly verified it for herself in a hundred and one ways. Anjali had a way of cajoling, as well as shouting at me, to get into the core of the experience of what was being churned out on the page. She recognised the true value of the journal and felt that it was a landmark on the subject of kundalini. According to her knowledge, it was the first time that the entire process of kundalini awakening had been depicted in such visual detail.

Slowly and steadily, she worked with me on the manuscript. Since it would be too voluminous to bring it out as one book, we decided that it should be spread over three volumes. With her knowledge of spiritual and esoteric subjects, enthusiasm and guidance, the first volume took shape bearing the title *Conscious Flight into the Empyrean*.

This was the title that arose in my mind when we completed work on the book. I looked up the dictionary for the meaning of *empyrean*; it defined the word as "high heavens." I resonated with this as my experience took me through several planes and levels of consciousness.

Once the editing was complete, the creative team at the ad agency wholeheartedly supported the venture by contributing their skills in its layout and design. *Conscious Flight into the Empyrean* was published in December 1999. Over the next few years, the three volumes would be published as *The Kundalini Trilogy*.

My children decided to have a book launch at the leading Crossword bookstore in South Mumbai. This was all so new for us, and there was a level of excitement tinged with a sense of trepidation about the outcome. Friends came together to lend

Justice M. L. Dudhat releasing my first book at Crossword

their support. I requested Guruji to be the guest of honour and formally release the book. It was good to see familiar faces in the crowd, including my mother and other family members, as well as that of Pandit Chandrakantji. I was overwhelmed at the number of people who showed up. All in all, it turned out to be a very satisfying experience.

Today, Anjali, known by the name of Sri Ma Amodini Saraswati, lives in Rishikesh, where she guides many spiritual seekers on the path.

BABA GAGANGIRI

Param Pujya Swami Gagangirinath Maharaj

Our small group continued to meet at least once a week. During one such meeting, we went through past-life regression sessions, which we would then recount and share with the group once we were done.

At one of these sessions, I found myself sitting on the bank of a river flowing in full force and swirling around some poles before continuing on its way. I saw all this with my third eye. A week or so after this incident, Anjali suggested that we visit her Guru Baba Gagangiri at his ashram in Khopoli on the outskirts of Mumbai. The purpose of our going there was to show him my illustrations and seek his blessings for the forthcoming book.

We reached there around ten in the morning, thinking that we would have Baba's darshan and then head back to Mumbai. However, before we could meet him, we received the message that he had asked us to visit his cave on a nearby hill, where he had practiced sadhana for years. Even though Anjali knew her way to the cave, we were escorted to the base of the hill. Once the guide left us, a dog joined us and led us up the rough path to the cave. However, we were not able to go right up to the cave as the entrance was blocked by a landslide from the recent heavy rainfall in the area. As a result, we had to turn back and come back down from the hill. We were then invited to partake of the food that was being served in a semi-open hall, with a river flowing by its side in full spate. I sat down on the steps and began watching its flow as it swirled around some poles that were stuck in the gushing waters. This brought back the memory of the past-life regression session. It was now clear to me that instead of a past life, I had jumped into the future that was yet to unfold.

By this time, I had become quite restless and impatient to meet Baba Gagangiri, but we were told that we could meet him only around four in the afternoon. When that time arrived and I showed him the folder that had the drawings of my experience, he looked at them with great interest, and he pointed at some of the drawings, indicating that he knew exactly what they were about. As he flipped through the pages, his face would light up every now and then, and he would point at something in the drawing. Then he would let out a happy laugh of recognition. As mentioned earlier, he was gracious enough to give a commendation for my first book, *Conscious Flight into the Empyrean.*

We had the good fortune to meet him on two or three other occasions. Ashish Bhai, who looks after the ashram, would act as the translator because Baba only spoke in Marathi. Baba had a high-pitched voice, a good sense of humour, and a cackling laugh. When he was meeting devotees, he was often found reclining on bolsters placed on a swing, which was as big as a bed.

My last visit to the ashram became a milestone in my sadhana. When I met Baba, he blessed me by placing his hand on my head. This led to my becoming a witness to the flow of breath in the body. Before this, I could never understand what was meant by the words "watch your breath." While meditating at home the next morning, my attention got focused on the breath, and the consciousness moved with it, going in different directions till it went to the base of the spine and shot through the sushumna, like a rocket at great speed. The thought that crossed my mind was *Pavan Putra Hanuman*, and the perception that followed was the insight that Hanuman is the symbol of breath. No wonder He is worshipped by everyone.

Receiving the blessings of Baba Gagangiri in 1999

I regard my visits to Gagangiri ashram as being very meaningful. Going there had set in motion a certain restlessness, impatience, and frustration that somehow dissolved after meeting him. The last visit helped rearrange the jigsaw puzzle of my body and mind and cleared the path for my breath to flow in a rhythm that was required for my spiritual journey.

Gagangiri Maharaj hailed from southern Maharashtra. At the young age of seven, he left home and went to a *math* of the Nath Sampradaya, a well-known religious sect that has establishments all over India. As a youthful sanyasi, he moved in the company of *mahants* in the Himalayas. During this time, he learnt yoga together with several occult and religious practices. He travelled far and wide and then went to live in a cave in Himachal Pradesh before settling in Mumbai.

His continuous meditation and austere penance helped him attain Self-realisation. As people started benefitting from his meditations, healings, and cures, they began worshipping him, and he soon attracted a large, devoted following.

Maharaj left his body on February 4, 2008. Today, his main ashram at Khopoli flourishes and continues to attract devotees. There is also a Nath Gagangiri Maharaj ashram at Malabar Hill in South Mumbai.

The deep connection with Baba Gagangiri continues through my daughter Shibani who is his ardent devotee. She organises regular satsangs and programmes for The Art of Living at the Malabar Hill ashram.

THE TRILOGY IS COMPLETE

In 2002, work began on the next part of my diary. The second book in the series was published as *Kundalini Diary*. Rohit Arya—who was already working with Gautam on some publishing projects, including *The Sacred India Tarot*—came on board as editor for this book.

In a certain way, Rohit introduced me to who I am. Reading his preface to *Kundalini Diary* gave me an insight into the work I had unconsciously produced, although it had all been recorded very conscientiously. After all, the first book was called *Conscious Flight into the Empyrean*. In the preface, Rohit wrote the following:

> To me, as a practicing mythologist, the primary attraction to this work was the many global mythic themes she had accessed. This book gave a possible answer to two core questions about mythology: Where do stories come from, and why do they take the shape they do? They come from inner experiences, from strong visual imprinting.

These lines made me look at all the illustrations with renewed understanding. His insights enabled me to get a deeper understanding of the subtle dimensions, while interpreting the visions and the play of vibrations and the shapes these dimensions can take.

It was Rohit's knowledge and understanding of the spiritual evolution of the soul that nudged my inner wisdom to surface when I assumed the role of a teacher. It is not the egotistical self that speaks at that moment; it is the guru within that takes over.

In 2005, the last part of my diary was brought out as *Kundalini Awakening,* the third book in the trilogy. Once again, Rohit helped me with this book, thus bringing the trilogy to completion. Working on it led Rohit towards his awakening, which transformed his knowledge into experience.

Interacting with Rohit during the course of working on these books helped me arrive at a final understanding of the knowledge revealed through my mystic experience. This work with him subsequently led to the publishing of two more books, *Who Am I?* and *The Eight Spiritual Breaths.*

With Rohit Arya at my residence

TAKING ON THE ROLE OF A SPIRITUAL GUIDE

The breaths, affirmations, and meditation had gently and gradually worked on clearing my mind so that the intellect could assimilate the knowledge that was pouring forth in the form of visions and sensations of the flow of energy. The breaths opened up different areas of the brain. The Brahma Vidya Course is designed with breaths and affirmations that systematically awaken and lead an intuitively receptive aspirant toward the Truth. The road map has been drawn; how long the traveller takes depends upon how conscious and aware he or she becomes of the gift that is being offered.

It was around 2004 that an urge arose in me to conduct a group meditation. I told Guruji that I wished to start my own meditation group at my home. He said I should go ahead and that he would support my endeavour. It felt wonderful, and I fixed the group meditation time on Thursdays from six to six thirty in the evening. Initially, about five of us would meet for a cup of tea and then sit for meditation. Since we were all friends, there was a feeling of relaxation and ease among us. As a result, we were all able to share our apprehension and fears connected with meditation. One friend was scared to close her eyes for fear of not knowing what would come up. Another found it simply boring to sit with closed eyes, and yet another would take out her mala to do japa. After a few weeks I decided that

Leading a group meditation in the outdoors

we would do a guided meditation with a music CD. This was a blessing as it not only put everyone at ease but also took them gently through the chakras in a systematic way. After a couple of months, the group felt comfortable and relaxed while meditating to music with closed eyes.

It was now time to start the silent meditation. I was wondering how to go about it. Should I just sit with eyes closed and expect that everyone would follow my lead?

What would Guruji be doing or thinking while he was leading a group meditation? So I asked Guruji, "When you sit for meditation, is there anything you say to yourself, or do you do anything? What should I do?" His answer was, "You do nothing. Just sit, and everything will be done." I followed the same pattern of meditation that was followed when we sat with Guruji. That is, he would look at each one of us, specifically at the centre between the eyebrows, and he would then instruct us to look at the same point between his eyebrows. Once this exchange happened with each aspirant, he would close his eyes, and then we would close ours. I felt this would connect the aspirant to the guru's energy, and those of us who were receptive would receive it. Guruji would chant an Om to signal the end of the half-hour meditation, and the others would follow suit by chanting Om in unison.

I became a keen observer of what was transpiring during the half-hour meditations. There were no thoughts arising in my mind; I would simply observe the flow of energy moving out from where I was sitting. It would either circle the group, or it would just remain present in the room. Sometimes, it seemed to be coming from another source toward me and then moving out through me into the room. In a few months, I found that it started to move in a pattern. I saw some aspirants receiving it, while it would bypass others. My understanding of the workings of the Force was getting better with successive weekly meditations.

I began to have a clearer understanding of the individuals who came for the group meditation. I could see who was relaxed, who was partially in the mind, and who was not present at all. With the coming of new entrants into the group, there came new challenges

Group meditation at my residence

and learning; these issues I had not experienced in Guruji's meditations. I came to understand the workings of the energy for each aspirant, depending on the chakra and issues involved. For those who were relaxed and surrendered to the energy, it would work faster by clearing blocks relating to any mental and emotional issues.

As more people showed up for group meditation, I emphasised that the practice needed to be regular. Meditation is not a one-day trip; it is a process of transformation, and it is ongoing. No mantra is given except to watch the inhalation and exhalation of the breath. It is the energy that initiates the process by transference of shakti through the guru.

Years of meditation with Guruji and conducting group meditation in my home have taken me through sadhana's different stages. Finally, I have come to the understanding that meditation is a state that is beyond thought, beyond the experience of waking, sleeping, and dreaming.

PAST LIVES: A WINDOW INTO PRESENT LIFE SITUATIONS

The breathing exercises and empowering affirmations that I practiced opened up areas of my brain, and the knowledge I gained, I put down in the form of a diary, which was eventually published as *The Kundalini Trilogy*. It decoded the latent potential of humans in a relatively simple way. The method was effective only if the seeker pursued it with awareness and dedication.

Whatever we manifest is actually stored in our minds, and the thread of life continues from where we left off in our earlier lives, moving us in this life toward working out our karmic issues. However, we do not know this at the conscious level. During our lifetime, if awareness arises, then we can approach these issues with understanding and adopt an attitude based on an appropriate response to a situation and not based on a knee-jerk reaction to a stimulus. This can help us work toward clearing most of our karmic baggage.

While looking at the illustrations of my past lives, the understanding of karmic patterns became absolutely clear to me. I observed that if one has deep-rooted fears—let's use financial losses as an example—these fears come from our past life or lives. These issues have not been resolved, and our debts remain unpaid during this lifetime. The fear persists that we have time and again gone through life after life with unstable finances, and so this anxiety about financial loss has taken deep root in the storehouse of our memory.

Fear of Horses

I feared horses so much in this lifetime that even though I loved and admired their graceful movements, I would not go anywhere near them. Strangely enough, I have always had sculptures of horses in my home.

I have seen myself as a soldier fallen from my horse. I was lying on the battleground with my right leg blown off, while the horse bolted with fright.

In an earlier lifetime, I have seen myself as a young woman in a carriage, drawn by two horses. The carriage went over a land mine, and we were all blown up. Both these incidents occurred in a European setting, and the people in the vision were wearing period European dress from hundreds of years ago.

In another life, as a young woman in her twenties wearing riding gear, I see myself riding a fine horse in the countryside. The horse canters at an easy pace and then gallops, until it trips over a rock, and both of us plunge headlong down a cliff.

In yet another lifetime, I am an Indian girl, dressed in a wedding gown. I seem to be marrying a European soldier in what appears to be a cathedral. This ceremony is followed by a traditional Indian wedding in a colourful setting, probably somewhere in Rajasthan. I see myself on the terrace of our house, from where I can watch the groom's *baraat* approaching. My bridegroom is astride a white horse, and as it draws nearer, I see him lift the *sehra* with his left hand, and I recognise his face as that of the man in the cathedral. There is a sudden burst of firecrackers. The horse panics, and the bridegroom is thrown off and gets trampled underfoot.

There was a difference from this last vision to the previous ones, in which I witnessed my deaths in earlier lives. Whereas my own deaths before left no impact or emotion, the death of my bridegroom tugged at my heart. Emotions of sorrow that were deeply embedded suddenly got released while witnessing the scene.

Balancing a Karmic Debt

Another episode in my present life that seemed unusual for a person of my temperament and background was having an interaction with an underworld godfather. This episode also bears resonance with my past-life regressions during meditation.

During one of these sessions, I saw a past life in which I am a young girl in a group of dancers, whirling around in a grand ballroom. I excuse myself from my partner and go out through the huge doors. I look down the wide steps with my hand resting on the railing to my right. I see a figure dressed in dark trousers, a long coat, and a tall hat, standing with both hands in his pockets. On seeing him, I run down the steps and come to a stop before him. We do not exchange any words. He takes out a small pistol or revolver and hands it over to me. I hide it in the folds of my gown and run back up the steps.

In this life also, I had to go through a similar situation, in which I had to seek the help of a godfather to recover the company's dues from a defaulting client. I managed to recover a small part of the total amount, consoling myself with the fact that maybe this amount was my karmic due. Therefore, I didn't fret about the loss.

Although these karmic patterns are repeated in some way or another in our lives, the heartening fact is that the good we do also comes back to us.

Connection with Tibet

My spiritual leanings and practices have also come from earlier lives. In one life, I perform sadhana in the cremation grounds. I am meditating, and a Tibetan monk is sitting at some distance behind me. In another life, possibly my immediate past life, I am practicing the ritual of *agni-snan*. It is a rite in which one takes the fire from the funeral pyre, puts it in a cauldron, and then pours the burning coals and ashes over oneself.

It is interesting to note that in this lifetime, the Brahma Vidya Course that I followed originated in Tibet, after which it came to India. It is, of course, a gentler system of spiritual evolution than the ones I followed in my previous lifetimes.

My Childhood Friend Tsundu

During the Tibetan influx in 1959, the two principal lamas that followed the Dalai Lama were Panchen Lama and Sakya Trizin Lama. Since my father was among the leading citizens of Mussoorie, we would invariably get an opportunity to be present when any dignitary was being hosted by the local municipal councillors at the Savoy or Hakmans hotels. Sakya Trizin was a somewhat stocky, moon-faced lama, who always smiled and who wore his hair braided in two thin plaits. He was always seen in a

Sakya Trizin with Khando Chazotsang (Fourteenth Dalai Lama's niece) in Mussoorie

maroon robe with a heavy shawl thrown over one shoulder. It was during a meeting with the Sakya Lama that I met a girl by the name of Tsundu, who was among his chief assistants.

Tsundu and I forged a close friendship during Sakya Lama's stay in a house on Camel's Back Road in Mussoorie. For me, it was exciting to have a friend from a different culture. As for Tsundu, she was happy to know someone in new surroundings and learn the ways of people in a world so different from hers. We would meet in the evening at a point in Library Bazaar and then go for a long walk sharing anecdotes with each other. She would tell me about the travails and trauma of their escape from Tibet. I could well empathise with their plight because it reminded me of the trauma of India's partition, which my parents had faced.

Tsundu introduced me to Tibetan food, which I found rather delicious. She also taught me how to make flat noodles and a staple Tibetan soup, with vegetables and eggs stir-fried in mustard oil. It's simple to make and a nourishing meal in itself, one which my brother, Shiv, continues to make and enjoy even to this day.

With Tsundu

To honour the bond of friendship, she even gave me one of her favourite Tibetan dresses, which fitted me perfectly, as we both were almost of same height. After her parents moved to Rajpur near Dehradun, I lost touch with Tsundu, but her memory has lingered on in my mind.

Padmasambhava

I joined the Brahma Vidya Course in August 1995. It was only after daily practice of the breath work for eight months that I was then given a *mudra* for meditation by an ascended master during one of my meditation sessions. In 2016, I came across a photograph taken of a huge statue of Guru Padmasambhava at a monastery in Sikkim. To my utter surprise, one of his hands depicted the very same mudra. This proved to me that we come into this life with the syllabus all ready and in place to be lived through. Every happening in our life has a map for it. This insight inspires awe and wonder at how life works itself out. We are always guided depending on how aware we are instead of getting entangled in the hows and whys of life situations.

The earliest recorded reference we have of the breaths in the Brahma Vidya Course dates back to over a thousand years. At that time, the University of Nalanda was a world-renowned Buddhist centre of learning. Padmasambhava (730 CE–805 CE), a great tantric practitioner and yogi, was then heading the Department of Yoga and Philosophy. According to legend, he foresaw the destruction of Nalanda by foreign invaders and, along with his chosen students, migrated to Tibet. His sacred teachings were a closely guarded secret handed down over generations through his chosen disciples.

Amongst his teachings was this set of powerful breathing exercises, which had been designed to help human beings realise their highest potential. These breathing exercises were mastered by Edwin John Dingle, a spiritual seeker from the West, who studied at the monastery in Tibet. He took on the name Ding Le Mei and brought this course back to the West, where he taught it to westerners as "Mental Physics." In Mumbai, Swami Ramanathan, after completing the Mental Physics correspondence course with Ding Le Mei, introduced it as Brahma Vidya.

The course's connection with Guru Padmasambhava makes me believe that I have been part of the lineage coming down from Padmasambhava for a number of lives. I once again came into the stream of the same lineage in this life, and all the while my journey was being monitored step-by-step by a Tibetan master.

Statue of Guru Padmasambhava at a Sikkim monastery

It is quite clear to me that my connection with Tibet runs deep, be it through the lineage of Padmasambhava, past-life recollections, being in the presence of His Holiness the Dalai Lama, or through the Brahma Vidya Course, which led to my awakening and subsequent spiritual journey.

Close-up of the hand of Guru Padmasambhava

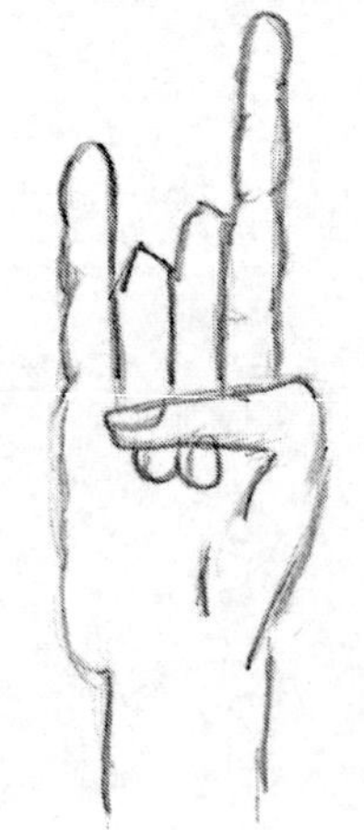

Mudra shown to me in meditation

SWAMI RAMANATHAN: THE EMBODIMENT OF LIGHT

My association with Swami Ramanathanji, whom I fondly called Baba, began in August 2000. There was an urge to meet him as he was the guru of my guru, and was responsible for bringing the Brahma Vidya Course to India. I hired a taxi and visited Ramanathanji in the distant suburb of Vashi. This was the first time I had ventured out on my own so far by taxi, but as luck would have it, the driver drove straight to the address I had given him.

Swami Ramanathan lived in a small flat on the ground floor, along with his wife, Chellammal. His daughter, Kalpana, lived in the flat opposite theirs with her family. From there, she could keep a constant eye on anyone coming and going from her parents' home and look after their daily needs, as they were quite old.

Baba was a tall man with a gentle face and childlike demeanour. I spent a wonderful morning with him, as I was made to feel welcome and fed with food and love. I became a regular guest at their home, visiting them once or twice a month.

During my first meeting with Baba, we talked in general about my experience with the teaching of Brahma Vidya. On my next visit, I took a shawl for him, and in subsequent visits, I would take some food along that he would enjoy eating, something different from his daily fare. He loved sweets but avoided eating them because he was diabetic.

I felt at home with the family, and we would often joke and have a hearty laugh together. My relationship with Baba and Maa was that of a child with loving parents. They looked forward to my visit. Perhaps I brought in a different energy than their regular visitors. There was no formality; love and joy would be flowing all around. In due course, my children also visited him.

On one of his trips to South Mumbai, when Ramanathanji was visiting some devotees, I invited him to our home and extended the invitation to include those who were accompanying him. It was an enjoyable lunch. After the meal, Baba rested for an hour and then left to go back to Vashi.

During one of my visits, I asked him what is the secret a guru shares with the disciple when the disciple is ready. His answer was, "What you did not know before and you know now is the secret." So simple.

Once, when I had gone to spend some time with them, Kalpana had to step out for an errand. It was left to me to serve food to Baba and Maa. It gave me a joyous feeling to be of some service to this divine couple. After I had washed the plates and utensils, Baba called out to me, and we sat opposite each other, while Maa went to rest. He entertained me with stories of his younger days and of his fleeting mystical experiences. I think Baba did this because he wanted to acknowledge my gesture and show his appreciation.

Gradually, I found out more about Baba's childhood and his life's journey, especially its spiritual aspect. I came to understand that Baba had the gift of *vaak siddhi*: if he thought, felt, or voiced something relating to a certain situation, it would manifest in some form or another. For example, if someone hurt Baba's feelings or had any intent to harm him or anyone connected to him (be it family or students), it would rebound on the individual concerned.

After hearing about a couple of such instances, I found it strange that the rebound effect would sometimes result in death. Baba seemed to narrate these incidents with a childlike wonder; for him, it was a divine happening. Once a buffalo hurt Ramanathan when he was just a toddler. The next morning, the buffalo was found dead. In another instance, a neighbour's daughter, who used to come to Baba's home so they could study together, mentioned that a certain boy would invariably misbehave with her on the train. Next day, the boy, while hanging from the doorway of the speeding train, was knocked down by a pole.

Baba was married to Maa at the age of twenty-three. He found employment in the steel industry in 1945 and was with the company for eighteen years. During this period, he experienced strange sensations in his body-mind organism. He consulted an astrologer in Madras, who predicted that after twelve months he would not work anymore. The astrologer also suggested he get a medical checkup. Ramanathan consulted a doctor who examined him and diagnosed pressure on the brain. He was advised to rest and abstain from work. But when his father passed away in 1967, the responsibility to provide for his mother and brother fell on his shoulders, since his father had frittered away the family's savings.

It was in 1968 that he realised that the physical and mental discomfort that he had been experiencing was the result of the activation of his kundalini energy. His understanding of kundalini deepened as he read books on the subject, particularly those by Pandit Gopi Krishna. During this time, he also took a correspondence course on Mental Physics, which was introduced to him in an article on light by Edwin John Dingle. John Dingle was an Englishman who, under much hardship, undertook a journey to Tibet. It is there that he studied a course on ancient

Edwin J. Dingle (Ding Le Mei)

The nameless Tibetan master, guru of Ding Le Mei

breathing exercises under a Tibetan master, whom he considered his spiritual guide. He then brought this course to the West and, using the name of Ding Le Mei (a name given to him by the Tibetan master), taught the course to aspirants as Mental Physics. He also enabled overseas aspirants to study it by offering a correspondence course.

The article stated that the course fee was twenty-three dollars, a sum Ramanathan could not afford as his salary at that time was only twenty rupees per month. Later, when he joined another organisation on a monthly salary of Rs. 175, he enrolled in the correspondence course.

Ramanathan was a keen aspirant and a true disciple of Ding Le Mei, whom he considered his guru. Noting the sincerity and dedication of his student, the guru waived the tuition fee for the advanced course, and Ramanathan then continued his spiritual progress by doing the preceptors' course. After this, Ramanathan made three visits to the headquarters of the Mental

Physics Institute in California. On one of these visits, he was given the title of Guru Jyotirmayananda, which means "the embodiment of light" in Sanskrit. The highest honour for him was later to be presented with Ding Le Mei's diamond-studded platinum ring and coat. On May 11, 1985, Ramanathan returned to Bombay and renamed the Mental Physics Course as Brahma Vidya and registered his mission as a charitable institute. He was elected founder and president of the mission and endowed with a monthly allowance.

Regular classes of Brahma Vidya began all over Bombay with the Mental Physics curriculum, consisting of a six-month initiates' course, a children's course of seven weeks, a two-year advanced course, and the preceptors' course of another two years. Hundreds of students completed the courses with Guru Jyotirmayananda, with some of them holding their own classes in Brahma Vidya at home and abroad.

In conversation with Swami Ramanathan at his home, in 2001

Baba would often mention a wish for a book on his life's journey. His devotees had not paid much heed to it. I did not know the full details of his life to do justice to it, but this being his keen desire, I suggested we talk about his life story whenever we met. I suggested we could make notes and assimilate them to see if they could develop into a book. This is what we did on my various visits, and our notes finally culminated in a book called *The Embodiment of Light*. I was glad that I had been able to play a role in getting his wish fulfilled.

The energy was active in Baba even during his last days. He would bring this energy to the awareness of his devotees by pointing to his eyebrows and the hair on his arms standing on end.

Baba left his body consciously in the year 2004. I went to see him one day before he passed away. Although he was very weak and could not speak, his eyes were open and alert to what was going on around him.

He has left us with the beautiful gift of the Brahma Vidya Course.

LAST DAYS WITH THE GURU

> Guru is pure effulgent spirit, the dispeller of darkness, the epitome of what each individual aspires to be. His domain is the spirit, and it is to guide us into this realm that he appears. Once the link with the guru is established, time cannot change it, nor death eradicate it. It is a permanent union. Guru stays with you life after life.
>
> —Swami Satyanand Saraswati

When I look back on my life, I can clearly see the play of Consciousness at work in my existence. Each soul is continually working toward a higher stage of evolution, which would normally entail the redeeming of past debts or karma. So it becomes apparent that we come into this world and into our karmic circle with a preplanned script. Everyone in the circle has an integral role in the drama, yet only a minute fragment of humanity is conscious of it. Most of us plunge headlong into life and are usually dissatisfied with the outcome.

When some of us go through the trials and traumas of life as a witness, with not much ego data to disrupt the play, then Consciousness supports us through life's intricate patterns, leading us from fragmentation to wholeness. If we press the replay button of our lives, we will see the interconnectedness of our life's events and how we are always supported in the choices we make.

Guru Consciousness

Guru consciousness exists in all of us and is known as the "inner guru." This inner guru is the witness of all that we do in life, silently guiding us on the path to knowledge of the Higher Self. Invariably, we are distracted and pay no heed to the guidance. Since the Self is the purest and subtlest element within us and beyond our comprehension, we unconsciously seek or come across someone who is a replica of our inner guru. It is said that when you are ready, the guru will appear to instruct you to remember what you know but have forgotten.

Having a teacher to guide us in any field is invaluable, more so in spirituality. As spirituality is subtle and intangible in nature, we need a guru who can bring to our awareness the universal spiritual principle. My unconscious search for such a friend, philosopher, and guide ended when I was led to my guru. In him, I found all that represents purity, peace, love, and wisdom. Under his guidance, the rough edges of my personality dissolved in due course to reflect new inherent qualities within me.

The relationship with my guru followed the traditional pattern, wherein the transmission of teaching from guru to shishya takes place through silence. In this relationship, there is not much verbal dialogue; subtle, advanced knowledge is conveyed and received through silence. However, in order for this to happen, the body, mind, and intellect have to go through a process of purification. The purification or growth occurs when faced with life situations. Much pain and anguish is felt because catharsis is required, and such situations will keep surfacing till one awakens from the dream world one has created and accepts Reality as is, without complaint or blame. The role of a guru is to shatter the illusions one is living under so that the Reality becomes available to us. His motives are selfless. He has the special ability to be part of everything and yet remain outside as a witness.

In 2006, my guru started to move in and out of the hospital because he was diabetic. Never for a moment did his demeanour give an indication of any stress or urgency; the weekly meditations at his home continued. It was in the month of July or August that Guruji stayed in his bedroom, while we would meditate in the hall. We would go meet him one by one before or after the meditation. In September, I had a dream that I narrated to Guruji, a story that made him smile when he heard it. In the dream, I saw him get up from his wheelchair, stand on his feet, and then walk into his room. He came back with a whole lot of medicine strips in his hand. He gave them to me, saying, "I am done with these."

Since I was living in the vicinity, I had been in contact with Guruji for the past ten years. Although there was not much interaction with him on a personal level, the relationship developed to a subtle level where I could intuitively sense a message or an instruction from him. With this sort of link happening between us, a new understanding and another way of looking at situations dawned in me. The result was that issues that cropped up were quickly clarified and would suddenly cease to be a problem. I realised that the same issue or situation was recurring until a time when I could understand that the situation was inviting me to look at a part of my own self that I had to work on. As soon as I stopped reacting to the stimuli, it would automatically drop.

My spiritual journey had taken a particular direction; the process of integration was still going on. When it became apparent that he had a limited time on this earth, the feeling of incompleteness, fragmentation, and abandonment in midstream began to surface.

We had stopped meeting for Tuesday meditation, as Guruji

was not comfortable enough to sit. As a result, we were clueless as to how he was feeling, and there was a desire among the group to know about his welfare. However, I was in touch with Uday, one of the four young men in the meditation group, over the phone, and I became aware of Guruji's overall health and spirit via his updates.

During this period when he was immobile, the four young men from the meditation group began keeping him company every evening, either by learning from him or by playing cards with him. On one such day, the group fell short of a person. Since I lived in the neighbourhood, I was asked to join the group. With this invitation, life fell into a pattern. As there were no visitors in the early part of the morning, I could keep Guruji company from ten thirty in the morning to noon or so.

Going through the brief notes I made after each of my visits, I noticed a peculiar pattern. Guruji would simply listen while I would talk and read out my notes to clear some doubts I had on Brahma Vidya. It was a one-sided dialogue on my part, and I would interpret the answer by Guruji's glance, nod, or a monosyllabic yes or no.

Here is my account of my visits for ten days to Guruji. These are exchanges of dialogue, verbal and nonverbal, that led to the completion of my spiritual journey.

September 11, 2006

Uday calls me from Guruji's residence to say that they are short of a person for the session of cards with Guruji. I go there, and we have fun playing *saat patti*. I was playing after a long time, and we were happy to see Guruji in an interactive frame of mind.

That night, I had a dream that the meditation group had gotten together. Guruji was sitting on his sofa, and I was sitting at his feet. When I narrated the dream to Uday, he said I should tell Guruji about the dream when I visited him next morning. It would make him feel good.

September 12, 2006

I enter Guruji's room with the greeting of "Good morning, Guruji!" He is lying on his back. I sit on the right side of the bed and gently and soothingly send energy to his legs and feet and take my cue from him when to speak and when to keep quiet. In due course, I start talking to him about *The Eight Spiritual Breaths*, the book I am working on, and read out the preface for his approval.

I then recall my dream of last night and happily narrate it to him.

"Guruji, guess what? I had a dream in the early hours of the morning! I dreamt we have come for meditation; you are sitting on your chair, and I am sitting at your feet. You suddenly get up and walk to your room, come back, give me some packets of pills and tell me, 'I have finished with them.'"

In a happy mood, I tell him that everything is going to be fine. He just smiles.

"Guruji, why are you not healing yourself?" I ask. He says, "A time comes when one has to stop doing and be in a state of being." He is silent, and it's wonderful to just be present in his energy field, which is broken now and then with spurts of conversation.

Touching his feet, I leave at twelve o'clock.

September 13, 2006

Guruji is awake and lying on his right side. I sit down on the bed and gently start sending energy to his legs and feet. After some time, he turns on his back. While talking to him, I go back to the time when meditation started at my home. I say, "Guruji, I remember the first day when you came to my house. I felt that God, in the form of my guru, had stepped in. There was a sense of elation and a boost to my ego. I felt highly privileged and special. Shibani, my elder daughter, was in awe and felt that our lives were going to change. Guruji, there are no words to express the gratitude and love that my children and I feel for you."

"These ten years with you have given a new and meaningful direction to my life," I continue, "And have paved the road ahead for my children, Shibani, Nikki, and Gautam. Guruji, thank you for your patience, love, and guidance. Even though I tend to slip now and then into non-awareness, I have on the whole learned to live consciously."

Holding his hand in both my hands, I say, "Guruji, thank you! Thank you! Thank you!" He has a beautiful and gentle smile on his face when I leave him.

September 14, 2006

It is Nikki's birthday. She comes along with me to get Guruji's blessings. As we enter the bedroom, we see Guruji sitting on the side of the bed with his feet on the floor. He is massaging his knees, looking a little pensive, but he is attentive to what we are saying. Nikki leaves after taking his blessings and giving him a loving hug and a kiss. I stay on, gently massaging his arms and knees. He seems more "there" than "here."

He is in a contemplative mood. To keep him attentive, I start telling him about my life in Mussoorie. I make him laugh when I tell him stories about the ghosts of Mussoorie and the prank one particular ghost played on me by waking me up every night at two in the morning. I also tell him about the time a young, goodlooking swami with blue eyes stopped by for overnight shelter. We made him sleep in my room without warning him of the nightly visitor. We keenly watched him the next morning for any sign that he would convey his discomfort, but he did not display any.

Whenever I break the silence, Guruji listens with a smile on his face and offers a comment, if necessary.

September 15, 2006

Guruji is lying on his back with a smile on his face as I walk in at eleven in the morning. His first words as I enter are, "You are late by ten minutes." I say, "Guruji, I thought I would give you time to settle." I realise my error, and henceforth see to it that I am on the dot for time. I sit down by his side, gently pressing his legs and rubbing his hands while we carry on a conversation. I say, "Guruji, when I look back, I find that most of the time, I have spent waiting. Waiting to get married, then waiting for the children to grow up, then for their education to finish and become self-supporting. Then waiting for them to get married and settle down. Guruji, does this waiting ever end? How long will this go on?" He listens attentively, but his response is short: "You are thinking as a mother."

I then narrate an incident, which happened a few years ago, that I had forgotten. I say, "Guruji, it is said that forgetfulness is a sign of good memory. How is that?" Then, we have a dialogue on memory. Guruji says, "Nothing is forgotten. A memory, no matter how old, whether deep-rooted or a surface impression, can get triggered at any time."

We also touch upon the subject of past lives.

September 18, 2006

On Monday, I took my Brahma Vidya Course book along.

We have a discussion about the negations and denials part in the book. I tell him, "Guruji, the negations in the meditation affirmations do not make sense to me. I think I will do without them in the book that I am working on." He says, "No! Understand and raise your consciousness while reciting them, and you will know why they should be there. They are the signposts that help an aspirant to know the state of his evolution." I answer, "Okay, Guruji. I will read them aloud, consciously and with awareness." He says, "I know them." I tell him, "Guruji, I would still like to read them aloud to you for my better understanding. You just relax and listen."

> Denial: Death is not a law of life. Man is not subject to decay, sickness, or old age. There is no old age. There is no decay. There is no death. There is no death. I am not subject to decay and old age. Now I am free, free, free forevermore…

Needless to say, by the time I am finished studying and reciting them with Guruji, my understanding of the negations and denials is enhanced, and my consciousness moves to another level. I later tell him: "Guruji, maybe I can explain the necessity of them in the book." To this he replies, "No, it has to be realised."

I leave with a greater understanding and a wider perspective.

September 19, 2006

I go with the third volume in the trilogy, *Kundalini Awakening*. I sit on the side of his bed and start a dialogue on Consciousness. My question is, "Guruji, how does telepathy work?" His answer is, "Unless you are at the same vibratory frequency, it does not work."

My next question: "Guruji, in the course of meditation, once the individual consciousness merges with the Guru Consciousness, is that a permanent state or a one-time happening?"

His answer, "It is a one-time happening. In order to achieve that state again, you have to raise your level of consciousness." He is pleased that I am no longer talking about kundalini and am more focused on talking about Consciousness. "Live consciously and in awareness," he says.

After some silence, I read an anecdote about a monk, which makes him smile. A smile is my reward, and I feel my mission is fulfilled.

September 20, 2006

When I enter, I find Guruji lying on his back. I sit by his side and start pressing his legs gently. Sensing his contemplative mood, I also close my eyes and start silently reciting my usual affirmation when we are quiet:

> The Creator is within me, looking at Guruji through my eyes. The Creator is within me, listening to the sounds of Guruji through my ears. The Creator is within me, thinking the thoughts of Guruji through my mind. The Creator is within me, healing Guruji through my hands. The Creator is within me, expressing through me... Whatever the Creator is, I am. I am that which It is...

I take Guruji's left hand and gently start running my hand over it. A most beautiful expression appears on his face, which is now glowing. I cannot contain my joy and tell him how radiant, happy, and beautiful he looks. He says a wonderful thing, and I feel blessed to be there to hear it. With that beautiful smile, he says, "My consciousness is serving you." I understand he is in a state of total identification with the Cosmic Consciousness, where there is no he, she, it, you, and me. All is One.

Then I tell him about the experience of a few aspirants from the previous day's meditation. I tell him that the collective consciousness of the group has moved to a level where there is gold dust. I say, "Razia and a few others felt that you were breathing through them. Guruji, it just shows that you are breathing to the rhythm of the cosmos, and as we identify with you, we associate that rhythm with you." Then I read him a quote from the book:

I sought Thee in the timeless halls of space
I sought Thee in the spaceless halls of time
But found that time and space do not exist.
I wondered 'Who am I?' and 'Who art Thou?'
And then I found Thee. Thou in me and I in Thee.
'Twas then I knew that I do not exist.
For I am nothing; yet am everything
For evermore...and so we cannot die.

—Robert Goslin, *Brahman*

By the time I finish reciting, he has gone back into silence. The sudden ringing of my mobile phone comes as a shock, and I run out with it, lest Guruji gets disturbed. It is my friend Meena. I have a few words with her and come back to the room. I find Guruji sitting with his head reclining forward in contemplation. He is gently massaging his knees. I sit down by his side and start running my hand gently over his back, shoulders, and arms. Feeling that he has lost weight around the shoulders, I say, "Guruji, you must eat properly. You are losing weight." He says, "I don't feel like eating. Every day, I have to take fifty-four pills and also two injections before food."

I get up and leave at 11:50 a.m. There is some hesitation to leave him in that contemplative mood. However, when I get up to leave, he tells me to call up tomorrow before coming as he will be going for some medical test. I give him a hug, kiss him on the forehead, and leave.

September 21, 2006

I call Uday at nine in the morning to check on what time Guruji is going for his test. He says the test was done, and they are on their way back. He says he will call me back later. I get his call around a quarter to ten, saying that the Doppler ultrasound exam was done, and the report would come on the next day. Guruji has gone in for his bath, and I can come at my usual time.

I go at quarter to eleven in the morning and find him sleeping on his side. Very quietly, I take the chair and sit at the foot of the bed, facing him. I slip into meditation. When I leave at the appointed time, he is still sleeping peacefully. I tell Anand, his man Friday, that I am going.

I come down and call Uday. I tell him that someone should look in on Guruji every half hour or so and gently bring him back from the silence that he drifts into.

When I call Uday in the evening to check on Guruji, he tells me that Ramesh, Nitin, Raju, and he met at the usual hour to be with Guruji. They were with him, and when it was time for his dinner, they all left.

September 22, 2006

According to Anand, Guruji got up at about two thirty in the morning to go to the toilet and then came back to his bed and slept. When he got up, it was usually his habit to sit on his chair in a meditation posture. But this morning, he lay down straight on his back, his hands folded on his chest. This is how he was found in the morning when someone went with a cup of tea.

Sometime in the early hours of the morning, Guruji had consciously connected with the Universal Intelligence.

THE EIGHT SPIRITUAL BREATHS

Once my experiences were published in my trilogy of books, I was curious to know what it all meant. So far, it had been more like taking a visual dictation, which had been presented in my awareness as drawings and diary notes. The time had now come to review, assimilate, and put down the deeper understanding I had gained so that it could benefit aspirants on the path of self-discovery. I went back to my original diaries, as well as the trilogy, while continuing my practice, until I gradually became consciously aware of the effect each of the eight breaths was having on the mind and the body and also of where and in what pattern the energy was moving.

I began making fresh notes. In due course, I understood the role of the chakras and how they become congested with unresolved issues of emotional distress, which act as blocks for the flow of energy, or prana. These blocks then surface as problems and illnesses that the body and mind has to undergo. With the practice of these breaths and their respective affirmations, the chakras get activated. In the process, some of the deeply embedded mental and emotional issues that block the chakras' efficient functioning are broken down and thrown out as toxins from the body. With the dissolving of some of the blocks, space is created for the awakened energy to move upward and to overcome any resistance that it may encounter in its path.

I observed my body spontaneously going through certain *kriyas*, which would not have been possible for me to do even if I tried with my own will. My breathing pattern would change or completely stop during meditation. I realised that all the recorded material had a greater meaning. A pattern began to emerge as each breath and its corresponding affirmation started working like a master sculptor chiselling away at the grossness of the body-mind organism to bring about a transformation. With this understanding, I learnt to relax and allow the process to take its course and complete itself, even when it came to erasing and reinscribing the grooves of my brain. Throughout this entire process, I began to understand the true meaning of surrender, which meant total trust and faith that whatever was happening was enabling me to reach the ultimate goal.

While noting it all down, I realised that a book was taking shape, one that would present the Brahma Vidya Course in a new light. I did not speak to Guruji about this until I had an absolutely clear understanding of the workings of the breaths and their affirmations at the physical and subtle levels.

Nowhere in the original Brahma Vidya Course book are the words chakras or kundalini mentioned. Guruji was also not in favour of my using these two words, which now and then I would use to express my experience. Perhaps these words were deeply rooted in my memory. Guruji was apprehensive that as these terms were esoteric concepts, the lay person would not understand them. Moreover, they were not everybody's experience. Those who have heard of kundalini have also heard about the fears and dangers associated with it, an issue which might also prove a deterrent to the path for some.

In the middle of 2006, once the initial manuscript was ready, I took it with me to the hospital when I went to visit Guruji, who was admitted there for a few days. Since I knew he was resistant to the word *kundalini*, I even quoted to him a paragraph from the advanced course of Brahma Vidya to support my inclusion of it:

> One who accepts tradition without independent personal thought does not perform any individual function in relation to human progress. He who accepts all the traditions of the past, subjects them to critical evaluation, and adds the benefits of his own experience is the true propagator of light and an important factor in the evolution of humankind.

The forthcoming knowledge had to be endorsed by him; otherwise, it could not surface as a new course book based on my personal experience and understanding.

It was only after his permission to go ahead that I seriously started working on fine-tuning the material for the book. This was finally published as *The Eight Spiritual Breaths* in March 2012, the month of Guruji's birthday and six years after he had passed away.

With the publication of *The Eight Spiritual Breaths*, my own understanding of the workings of the breaths at the mental, emotional, and physical levels has developed even more over the years. In the students who are committed to the course contained in *The Eight Spiritual Breaths*, I have noticed great health benefits: Improved memory retention, enhanced creative potential, increased states of calmness, and revitalised health and energy levels. This does not occur overnight but is an ongoing process of transformation at every level—mental, emotional, and physical. *The Eight Spiritual Breaths* is now also offered as an online course so that aspirants the world over can gain access to it.

OTHER BOOKS FOLLOW

The Kundalini Trilogy acted as an eye-opener for students and aspirants on the path. I began getting letters from seekers all over the country. Some expressed their confusion on certain aspects of kundalini awakening, while others sought clarifications on certain experiences they themselves were undergoing. Although they were receiving validation of those experiences through the trilogy, they still had some questions and doubts.

I realised that answers to questions raised by some of them would be of help and value to others who were having similar experiences. These questions were then collated into two volumes, titled *Kundalini Meditation—Questions and Answers Vol. 1* and *Vol. 2*. These two volumes also supported students of *The Eight Spiritual Breaths*. As general advice, I always tell students not to ignore any visualisations or kriyas that occur during these practices; they are the signposts and indicators of one's growth and evolution.

Another book I wrote, not quite related to kundalini, was *Sacred Flames*, which was published in January 2010. This book was co-authored with Rohit Arya, who once again brought the depths of his insights, this time to the significance of yajna fires. During a yajna, when the mantras are being chanted, the flames rise from the sacred fire and create semblances of the forms of various gods, goddesses, as well as symbols regarded as sacred to

Hindus. Some of these semblances were photographed as they arose from the flames and then reproduced in this book. Writing the book led to my realisation that the mantras being recited have the power to invoke the form of the deity being propitiated and worshipped during yajnas. I then knew how important it was to be consciously aware of what I say or the words I use in my daily interaction with people. I now also understood why Guruji insisted that I use the correct word to convey what I meant. This, of course, holds true for all of us.

In the final analysis, *The Eight Spiritual Breaths* brought me to the awareness of the question: Who am I? This was the subject of another book of mine.

Published in 2015, *Who Am I?* helps one understand that when one makes a wish or expresses a desire, the subconscious mind starts to work by preparing the body-mind organism to work toward the wish or desire. The book thus outlines the process the subtle body goes through to actualise a wish. In my case, the wish was to know the answer to the question about my own true identity: Who am I?

Once these books came out, letters started to come in from people all over the world who were following various techniques or forms of healing and yoga for self-development. Many of them stated that by just looking at the illustrations in these books, the energy got triggered in them, which led to different experiences and deeper insights. It was clear to me that the drawings were acting as the guru, bringing about whatever they were meant to in aspirants who resonated with them. They were guiding them through their process of evolution and validating their experience.

With this feedback, the thought arose of bringing out one book that would encompass the entire visual journey that had originally been spread out over three volumes of the trilogy.

This was now published as *The Kundalini Artworks*, a large format, hardcover book, in which only my illustrations were reproduced without any of the supporting text present in the trilogy. Through the sequence of these illustrations, *The Kundalini Artworks* visually outlined the process that the body, mind, and intellect go through to discover the abode of the Source, which resides in the human body in the form of the spiritual heart.

The reason why the illustrations were reproduced without supporting text was so that they could be seen and meditated upon in their pristine state. They would then create the desired impact upon the viewer—to serve as guideposts to one's journey.

As mentioned earlier, in the past I would often be told, "It is your experience, so how will it help others?" Now I know my experiences and understanding gained have helped many on the path. All in all, it has been well worthwhile. My approach to life has reminded me of Robert Frost's "The Road Not Taken":

> Two roads diverged
> in a wood, and I—
> I took the one less
> travelled by,
> and that
> has made all the
> difference.

GURUNATH: THE KRIYA YOGA MASTER

My son, Gautam, came in contact with Yogiraj Gurunath during the course of editing a manuscript by one of Gurunath's disciples, which was eventually brought out by our publishing house. After this, Gautam assisted Gurunath in publishing his own book, *Babaji: The Lightning Standing Still*, which is on Mahavatar Babaji, the Deathless Master.

During the course of their interactions, they developed a mutual bond of respect and affection. I accompanied Gautam on one of his visits to Gurunath. Gurunath's ashram has a rustic look, situated as it is in a forest-like setting about an hour away from Pune. We sat outdoors in a small yet cozy semicircular area. Gurunath was sitting on a big, cushioned chair-like seat, while visitors sat opposite him in a semicircle.

Gurunath has built a temple within the precincts of the ashram at a slightly elevated area on the hillside. A unique feature of this temple is that it has a lingam made of solid mercury. It is a quiet space where people sit and meditate around the lingam. He asked us to visit the temple and spend some time there.

Gurunath has a powerful persona, like the rishis of a bygone age. When I set my eyes on him, I recognised him as the rishi I had seen in a vision at the shrine of Shirdi Sai Baba during the evening aarti on one of my visits there. In the vision, I saw a look-alike of Gurunath moving around Sai Baba and collecting fresh flowers in a haze of incense smoke.

It was a comfortable meeting for me as Gurunath was an easy person to be with. The next morning, I had the opportunity to spend some time and show him the books about my experiences of kundalini. He went through them with keen interest.

A few years after this encounter, my book *The Kundalini Artworks* was published. When it was ready to go to press, I asked Gautam to see if Gurunath would be open to writing a few lines for the book. My son was skeptical, as Gurunath did not generally endorse other writers' books. Hence, it came as a joyous surprise when I received a most appropriate message for the book from Gurunath, which is included within its initial pages.

After this, I briefly met Gurunath twice, once at his house in Pune city and another time along with Gautam at a hotel's poolside coffee shop. It was nice to see him in casuals and looking handsome, with his silky beard, shoulder-length hair, and Nath symbol of *baalis*. A hotel guest came over to our table and said to

Presenting Yogiraj Gurunath the first copy of *The Kundalini Artworks* in 2015

Gurunath, "You look like Santa Claus." This was in the month of December, when Christmas decorations adorned the coffee shop. Gurunath looked up at him and replied, "What makes you think I am not?"

The last time I visited the ashram, Gurunath sportingly demonstrated for me a few exercises I could do to get relief from the stiffness in my back.

Like Gurunath, all the spiritual masters I have met or known are quite open and giving of themselves. If one is also open and receptive, their Grace flows freely.

THE FAKIR AND THE PIR

It was on one of my annual trips to an Ayurvedic centre in Coimbatore that I had met a Kashmiri couple, Tasavar and his lovely wife, Roohi. Living in the same complex for over a month, we became quite friendly and, on parting, they invited my family to visit them when we were next in Srinagar. In 2011, we decided to go to Kashmir for a holiday. When I contacted Tasavar, he told me that Roohi and he were in the United States but insisted that we visit his home in Srinagar and meet his sister and parents over tea. Knowing about our leanings towards spiritual masters, Tasavar told us to go and meet Qadir Sahib. It was decided that on our way to Pahalgam next morning, we would visit Qadir Sahib, who lived at a place called Aishmuqam, which was just twenty kilometres before one reached Pahalgam. As we were not familiar with the formalities required for meeting a fakir, Tasavar's sister Susan graciously offered to accompany us and serve as our guide and interpreter.

The first meeting was a little awkward because we were quite unfamiliar with the etiquette we needed to observe in a traditional Muslim setting. We sat down in a hall that had a low partition in the middle. On one side, there were men sitting in their Kashmiri garb, and on the other, were the traditionally dressed women, who had all come to seek Qadir Baba's blessings. He was sitting on a raised seat at one end of the room and smoking a *hookah*.

When Susan introduced us to him, Baba said we all must have food and then go. He then left the room. About half an hour later, we were asked to come out of the hall. It was sunny outside. Rugs had been laid out on the ground, and we were invited to sit there. The food was brought out by attendants, and Baba served us food that he had partly cooked himself.

During the delicious meal, Baba made it a point to sit for five minutes with my children, Gautam and Shibani, He mostly asked about their work. When it was my turn, I said, "Baba, please pray for me and my family." Baba replied, "You pray for me." I asked, "Baba, what can I pray for you?" He promptly answered, "Pray that I get funds to repair and extend this small and humble abode."

Back in Mumbai, I was narrating our meeting with Qadir Sahib to my meditation group. The next day, one of the ladies in the group called to say that, although she normally donates to the *dargah* next to her building, this time she would like to give her donation to Qadir Sahib and his home. I had only narrated the incident, not asked for any donation. Somehow, the word went around, and I soon found money coming in. Not knowing how much funds were required, Gautam phoned Baba's adopted son to ask about it. On hearing the amount, I found, quite to my surprise, that the entire amount had already been collected and was ready to be transferred to their bank account.

Later, when we were at a shop in Pahalgam looking at some shawls, the significance of this first meeting with Qadir Sahib dawned on me. The shawls reminded me of a dream I had one week before going to Kashmir. In the dream, I was told that I had to give a *chaddar* to a devotee of Sai Baba of Shirdi. Remembering this dream, I thought of Qadir Sahib's hall where we had sat. Lined high above on the wall were framed photos of various fakirs or seers, one of which was a photo of Sai Baba. When Baba sent a guide with us in the car to the shrine atop Aishmuqam, he informed us that just as people would go for healing to Sai Baba, people from around the neighbouring areas came to Qadir Sahib. He then added, "In fact, he is our Sai Baba." Suddenly, it struck me that I should give a shawl to Qadir Sahib and to no one else. We selected one shawl for Baba, and on our way back to Srinagar, we dropped by at his place to put the shawl around Qadir Sahib's shoulders.

Whenever we went to Kashmir, a visit to Qadir Sahib became a must. Even though we did not understand his language, the love he poured on us overcame any language barrier. He would send us off with apples and dry fruits after kissing our foreheads and eyes. We were always treated with a special courtesy: we were often served snacks with *kahwah*, the famous Kashmiri tea.

On one of our visits a few years later, he proudly showed us how the donations I collected had been used to extend the kitchen that feeds hundreds of people on special occasions. It is so

With Qadir Sahib at Aishmuqam near Pahalgam

empowering to be in the energy field of masters who give of their love in abundance.

Shafi Baba, a Sufi master, was introduced to Gautam by his friend in Pune. Meeting and knowing Shafi Baba is an experience in itself. He has a shop at one end of Dal Lake in Srinagar. The shop has all that one is looking for as a tourist: Kashmiri clothes, shawls, handbags, and other assortments. It was easier to communicate with Shafi Baba as his language was peppered with a smattering of Hindi. He took us around to different dargahs and mosques and gave us their brief history.

On one visit, when Gautam had donated some money to Baba, he asked us to come by early next day to his shop. When we reached the shop, we saw Baba loading a big bundle of clothes into the car's boot. He asked us to get into the car and took us to an orphanage for young girls and boys. When we got there, he asked Vilas (my son-in-law) and Gautam to help him distribute some clothes to the children. It was touching to watch Baba, the love and compassion he felt for all the orphans there. His love also encompasses the birds he feeds across Srinagar on a weekly basis. We also discovered that, once a month, he would rent a bus and take poor school children on a picnic.

Shafi Baba is a familiar face at the holy places in Srinagar, as well as in some towns nearby where people greet him as "Badshah." He is also a healer, though his healing method can be quite unconventional. As part of his healings, he may give you a powerful thump on your back, which will probably knock you over with its force. People bear the force of it for the healing that, more often than not, subsequently follows. I had a taste of Shafi Baba's healing touch when he took us to a botanical garden for a picnic. Having spent many years in the forests, his knowledge of plants and their healing properties is vast.

That day, I was complaining of a stiff back. He asked me to lie down on my back. Then, without warning, he gave me a sharp whack on the soles of my feet. Baba is a reasonably tall and well-built man, and he had whacked my soles with his *chappal*. His strike was so hard that it probably shocked the stiffness out of my body. He then ordered me to get up and run on a narrow path. I managed to run up and down the path, even though I hadn't run for several years or maybe decades.

There is a certain bond that has developed with Qadir Sahib and Pir Baba Shafi that gives a deep sense of belonging. Visiting Kashmir is like going back home to Mussoorie. The flowers, the mountains, and the clean, pure air are so invigorating. Kashmir is a powerhouse of spiritual energy as it is also the home of *Kashmiri Shaivism*. We are indeed fortunate to have received the blessings of these two saintly beings there.

With "Badshah" Shafi at his shop in Srinagar

AS I LOOK BACK

I have gone through life's journey donning the mantles of a daughter, wife, mother, businesswoman, aspirant on the path, and mentor and guide to seekers on their journey of self-discovery. I realise that if one goes through life as a robot without living in awareness, the action-reaction process is like any other involuntary action going on in the body. In other words, life is an automatic functioning of stimulus and response in daily living. Every morning, we start from where we left off the previous day.

My understanding is that in all probability, before taking rebirth the individual ego chooses the genealogical history of the family in which it wishes to take rebirth. It then becomes a part of that family tradition, which enables it to work towards completion of its life's purpose from where it had left off in the previous birth.

This is the basis for the ego's further evolution once its life's journey is set in motion. It goes through different phases of growth, engaged in routine, day-to-day needs and activities of life, interwoven with challenges that come its way. In the course of one's journey, if the individual has moved on to the spiritual path, then his or her life is given direction by the guru principle.

Having chosen the environment for my present life's journey, I now understand why I would always say that life has been lived through me. There has never been any major want or desire or the will to achieve goals. I realise now that if one's personal will does not come in the way, then one goes through good times as well as bad adopting a balanced approach, accepting each situation as a part of growing. This attitude arises because the active guru energy is guiding and providing support at every crucial stage. In my case, it kept nudging me in the direction I was to finally take when I came up with the question, "Is this life?"

This question arose within me when I handed over the reins of running the business to my son, Gautam. It had most likely been lying dormant in the subconscious and then had decided to manifest itself, thus providing me with the means to further enhance my spiritual growth. This came in the form of the course on Brahma Vidya, with a guru who would be my friend, philosopher, and guide for completing my journey and fulfilling the purpose of my life.

The ten years I spent in the energy field of my guru provided me with the experience of awakening to the knowledge of my enquiry, "Who am I?" and "Where do I come from?" This process brought with it certain issues of insecurity, rejection, and impatience, which surfaced during the journey. A major insight was the misconception that I was a patient person. In reality, my patience was a camouflage for impatience, be it with a person or a situation. This characteristic trait of impatience would lead to extended periods of dealing with undesirable situations.

My learning and growth occurred through keen observation of the guru and his interaction with the aspirants, together with my own self-analysis. It was interesting to note that he never criticised, blamed, or judged anyone. He went through his weekly lectures and meditations without ever admonishing aspirants for missing the sessions. His acceptance of us and our fluctuating behaviour patterns was without an iota of disapproval. Being in his space, one dropped all pretence and felt free to be oneself. He never offered advice unless one asked for it.

I came to my own understanding as to how it all came naturally to Guruji to accept everyone and everything "as is." It was from him that I imbibed the teaching of accepting everyone in my sphere as they are by understanding that we all come with our preplanned script, in which we have allotted the role and the dialogue for each player. Thus starts the play of Consciousness, of action-reaction situations, and of the subsequent struggle through life, because sometimes the scripts don't match and the dialogues clash. When wisdom dawns, one is content to watch the play without interfering. We allow each one to grow and evolve at their own pace. This learning happens only through constant awareness over lifetimes.

If someone were to ask me how my life has generally been, my immediate response would be that it's been quite smooth. This is because when I review my life, I see how it has progressed toward its final goal.

It started with my taking birth in a desirable family structure, in a family that had to go through its collective karma of being uprooted from its homeland, of being stripped of its inheritance, and of being forced to migrate to the foothills of the Himalayas. Later, it involved going through the loss of my husband, bringing up three young children, and sitting in the chair as the head of the advertising agency without a clue as to where I was to start from, meeting challenges at every step, suffering losses and the trauma of court cases, and dealing with the mafia. Somehow it seems quite challenging as I look back. The reason I managed to go through these stressful years with equanimity was and still is because we as a family have been under the protection of the guru principle. This has enabled me to lead a good and peaceful life.

Why do I think that each life has an end purpose? Take my life, for example: I understand now and accept that if I had not gone through the stress, hurts, rejections, and traumas at different phases more or less unconsciously (without questioning the how and why of it), that would not have tested my peace of mind. Fortunately for me, my mantras kept me in balance and helped me to grow through every situation. The realisation also dawns that if the stresses and traumas were not there, growth would not happen, and compassion would not develop.

Life is nothing but the play of Consciousness fulfilling Its own need through Its embodiment. Its purpose is to keep solving Its own riddle and to work through the pattern It has set for Itself. My role is to support It in whatever way I can in Its endeavour to move toward Its ultimate goal.

Its role for me is very clearly defined now—that of being a guide to those aspirants who are awakening to the energy lying dormant in them. Some are awakening through different forms of spiritual practice, through different breathing techniques, yoga, or japa. I find that it is not only the energy aspect that has to be addressed in aspirants; it is their whole life and family structure that must be taken into account as well. It is said that if one person from a family comes to the spiritual path, seven generations gone by and seven in the future benefit from it. I have seen this shift happen with my regular group of aspirants.

The process for the aspirants starts through contemplation and discipline. In due course, a shift takes place in attitudes as well as in their understanding. The realisation dawns that the situations that were stressful earlier are no longer there now. Just changing the way they communicated brought about a shift in the response they were getting from a situation or in their relationships. After years of their practice, peace, calm, and harmony finally prevails. The children grow up more balanced. Everyone responds instead of reacting. This then follows through each successive generation.

APPENDIX A

SELECTION OF DRAWINGS FROM THE KUNDALINI ARTWORKS

Note: Some of the drawings that appeared in colour in *The Kundalini Artworks* have been reproduced here in black and white.

Vibrations of ajna chakra

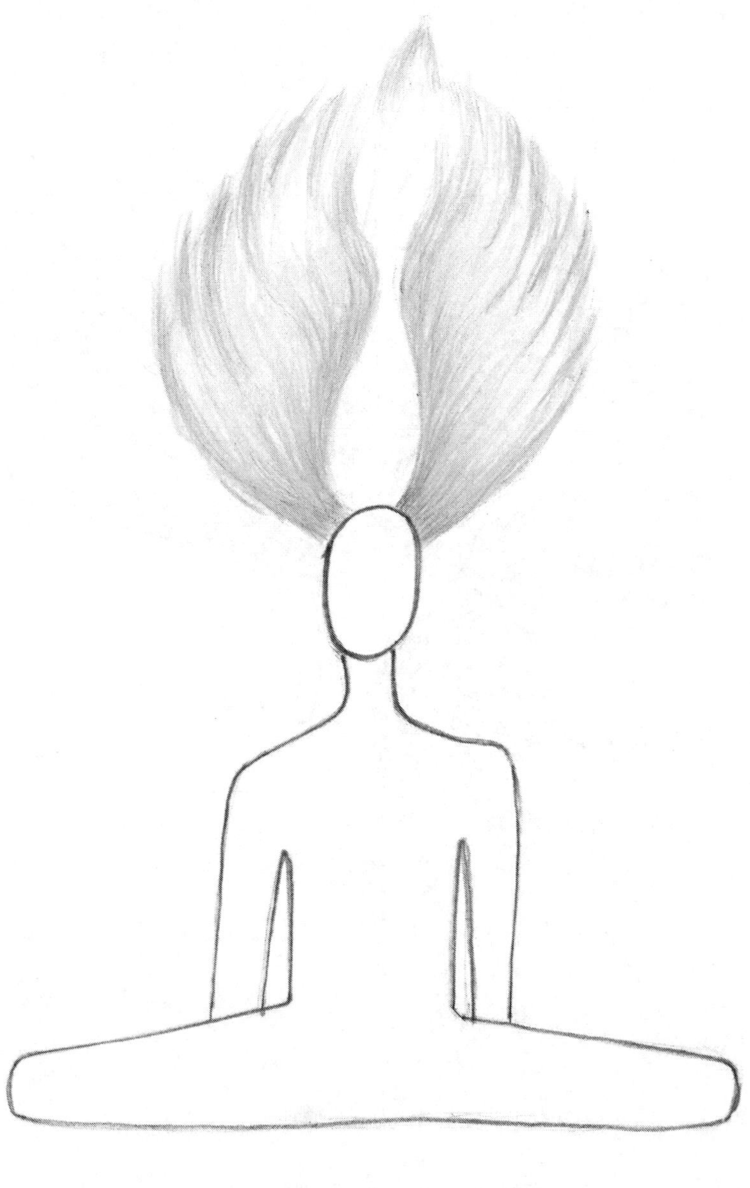

Wings of ajna chakra (vibration)

Glorious light radiating from anahata chakra, the spiritual heart

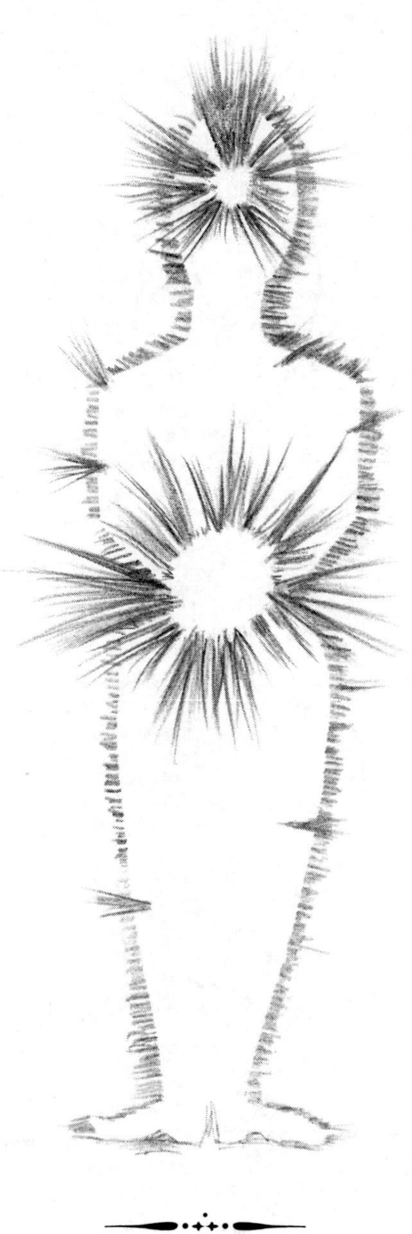

Active ajna chakra and manipura chakra

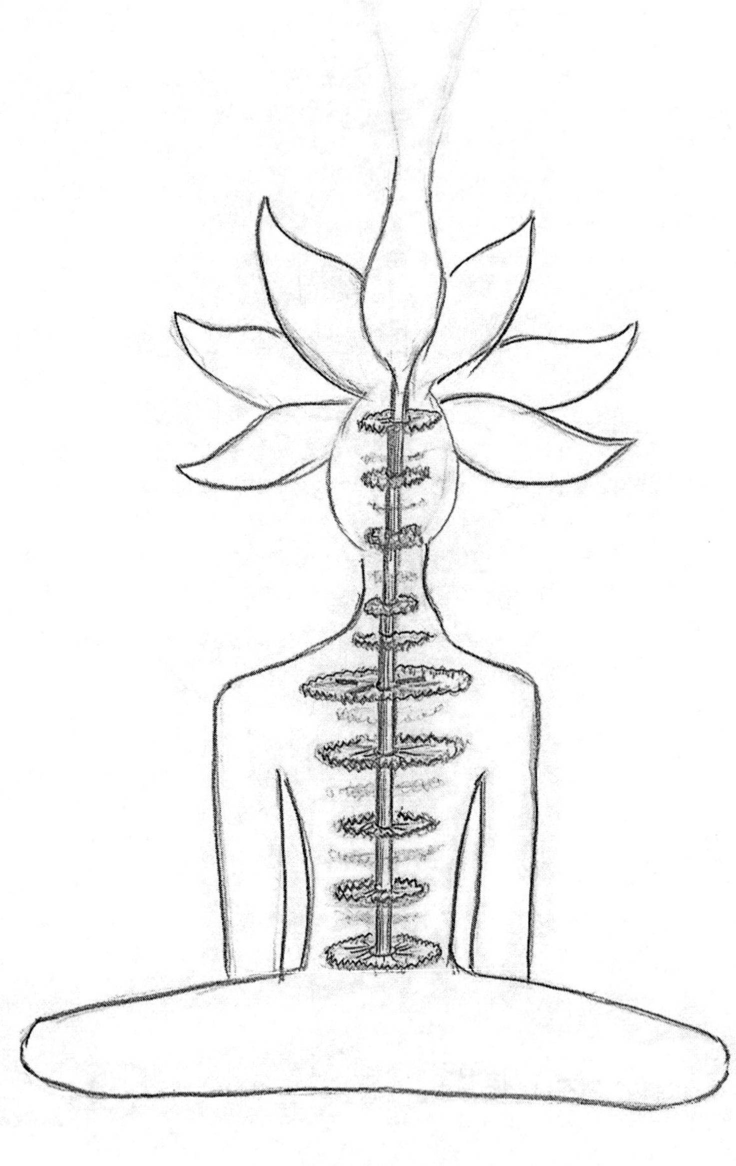

Flowering of sahasrara

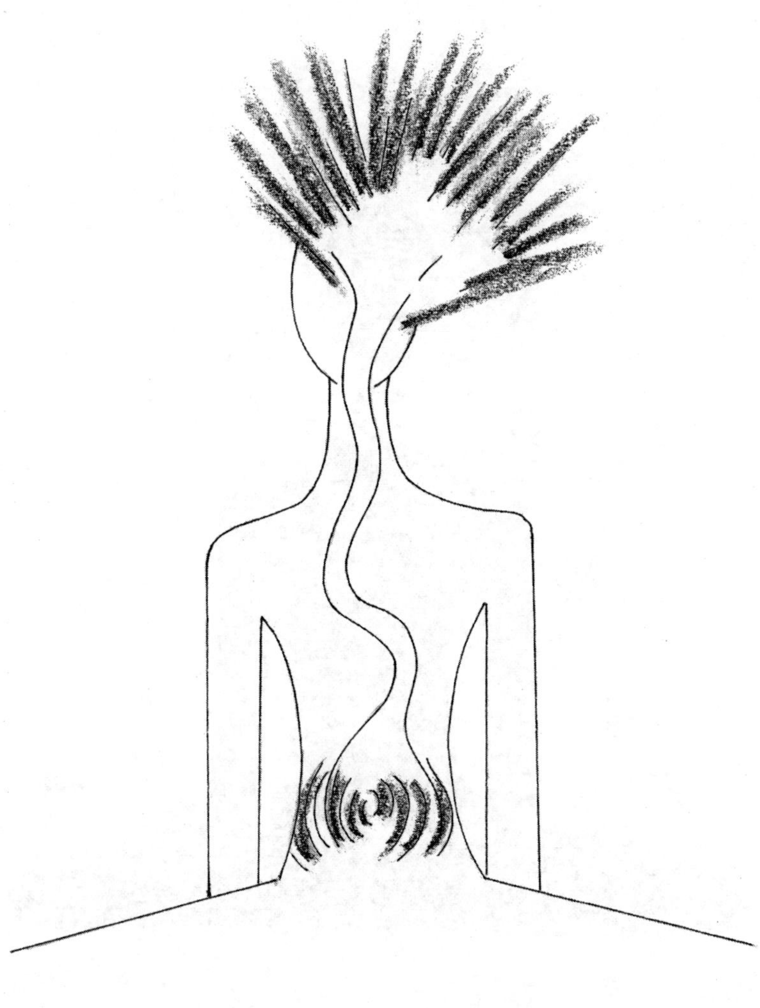

Ajna chakra and manipura chakra working in unison

Sutratma—the thread that binds all the selves in a human being

Flow of prana

On the wheel of karma

Contraction of the subtle body

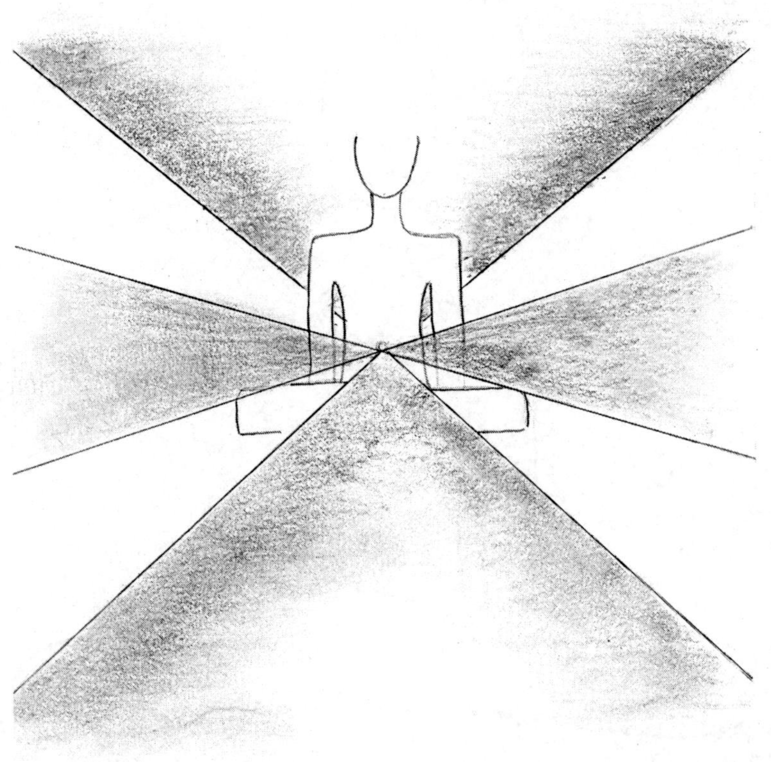

Expansion of the subtle body from the manipura chakra

Expansion of consciousness into the void

The subtle body fragments into silver particles

Silver particles of the subtle body move out into the void

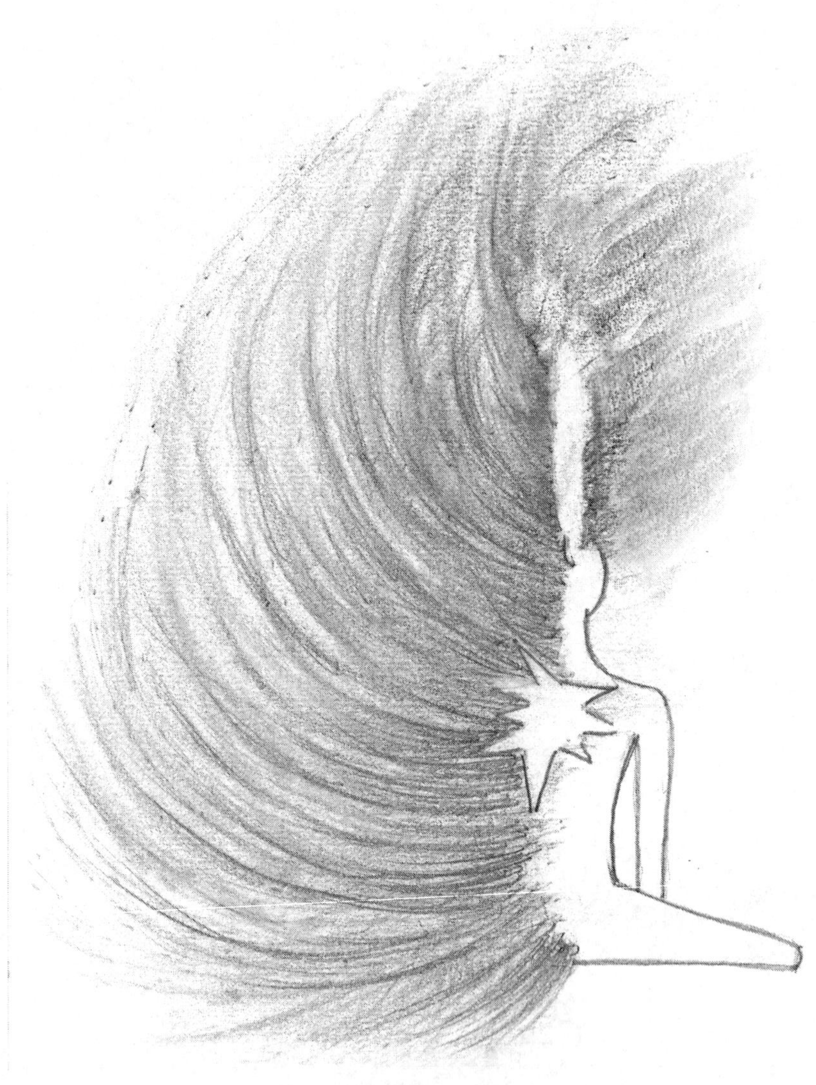

The subtle body merging with the cosmos

APPENDIX B

WHAT IS AN AFFIRMATION?

When we keep repeating or dwelling on a thought or emotion, be it negative or positive, it means we are affirming it. We do not realise that we are affirming and, by doing so, creating our life experience with every word or thought. Constant repetition of positive thoughts, emotions, and statements are released into the collective consciousness that shapes our future.

The affirmations in *The Eight Spiritual Breaths* have their origins in ancient scriptures. They are empowered with mantras and have been translated into English. In effect, they help expand awareness. If one is attentive to the affirmations, he or she will understand that they are designed to reveal, in a subtle way, how consciousness functions. This allows the unfoldment of consciousness to take place effortlessly within the individual.

By reciting the affirmations after the breaths, an opening is created, consciously and subconsciously, for a higher understanding to start descending into the individual consciousness. A deep state of calmness, an atmosphere of trust, and an openness to receive the unknown is also created by the one who affirms. This state of calmness, and the subtle understanding gained, helps in creating a more stable and trusting environment for the natural unfoldment and manifestation of the higher energies. The meditation affirmations, which are recited after all the eight breaths have been completed, are designed to take this process forward.

Without these affirmations, an individual's life is like a ship having the necessary fuel and power but no rudder to steer it. As a result, a person's life drifts aimlessly in the ocean. Thus, the affirmations play an invaluable role in directing the individual's unfoldment. They prepare the foundation and are like the banks of a river directing its flow so it can, on completion of its journey, merge with the ocean.

Similarly, the eight breaths and their affirmations expand the consciousness and allow individuals to actualise their full potential and ultimately move toward Consciousness as a whole.

APPENDIX C

DISCIPLES' ACCOUNTS AND EXPERIENCES

Rohit Arya

The kundalini awoke in me because of the drawings. The kundalini rises when people undertake spiritual practices, when people do kriyas, when they meet powerful gurus, or when they have some accident of fate that lets it loose. I was activated by drawings. This must be unique in the annals of Kundalini Yoga.

When I was asked to take a look at Santosh's drawings and notes, which were to be a sequel to *Conscious Flight into the Empyrean*, I had no idea what was in store for me. My world was about to be turned upside down and then flipped repeatedly.

I was quite knowledgeable about religion, spirituality, mythology, and so on, and I was asked to see if I could make some comments on the books that followed, which could set the drawings in a universal context of archetypes and shared human consciousness. I agreed, simply because the first book was an astonishing wonder to me.

In the entire history of kundalini, there has never been anything like this trilogy of books. In the past, people have written much about it, and there have been many diagrams depicting it, usually of the chakras and the nadi systems. But this work was beyond all expectations. Day by day, drawing by drawing, the entire process of activation, cleansing, and transformation was laid out in the book in an astonishing road map. Again—and I cannot stress this enough—there has never been anything like it in extant literature for over two thousand years.

This book is a breakthrough in how humans will engage with the whole context and system of Kundalini Yoga. It was dizzying then, and one still feels light-headed when one sees all the drawings in sequence. An inner reality that is beyond words has somehow been communicated in symbolic, figurative, and archetypal manner. The drawings were pared down to an instinctive minimalism;

there is nothing superfluous in them. They are simply just pure transmission. I made the enormous blunder of considering this to be information when it was shakti, the fiery lava of the Mahashakti Herself, and I was standing waist-deep in Her path. The old man was finished, and I had no idea my life was changed forever. All of this is hindsight, which is always perfect.

Although I was interested in spirituality and had a pretty deep knowledge of many matters, I had no sadhana, no spiritual practice, and no practical experience of things I had read about. So in the beginning, I did not comprehend that the mind was being stilled just gazing at these drawings. I would blank out for hours, even days, and it was most enjoyable. I was missing deadline after deadline to submit the manuscript back with my comments, but I was in its grip and really had no idea what was going on. Santosh and her son, Gautam, must have suffered a lot of irritation from my dilatoriness, but I was not in a position to comprehend or even recognise it. The more I pored over the drawings, the more things began to happen inside me. My entire internal reality underwent a revolution with this stimulus, and when it broke out, it was intense.

Kundalini activation need not be a fierce or painful process. That is a myth. In some rare cases, there is a lot of karmic residue or blockage that needs purging so that the shakti can do its work. When it encounters resistance, the shakti flares up and burns it out. Classically, there are supposed to be 186 signs and symptoms of kundalini awakening. I must have displayed about 150 of them at the very least. It was a fierce outburst, a volcanic eruption, but as I said, that is not really the norm. Too much fear mongering has gone into this. What happened to me was that because I had a destiny to be a guru in my turn and since I had not done any sadhana and I was already past thirty, the shakti had to adopt energetic measures! I had enough knowledge to recognise what had happened. It is solely the Grace of Nataraja that I did not waste this *avasaram*, this moment of karmic opportunity when all things change.

Reeling with the incalculable power throbbing within me, I went to Santosh and announced that this change has happened, and I told her that she is my guru. She was not at all pleased, mainly because my nature was and remains rather irascible. She also did not consider herself to be a guru figure, nor did she want the whole jamboree that goes with the title. Not at all disheartened by that flat out refusal to be promoted to discipleship, I merely remarked that whether she wanted it or not, her book has activated me so that I am in full-blown process. Insofar as I am concerned, she is my guru. And that was how my guru got her first disciple; I basically refused any other option.

She then told me to learn and practice the eight spiritual breathing techniques, which is the core sadhana of our *parampara*, and I was off like a rocket. That is another story altogether.

Sometimes I joke that *The Kundalini Trilogy* is the senior guru because merely handling and viewing the drawings can compel a person to the path of Yoga, even against their inclinations. What I will say next will sound like the usual disciple praise. But the truth of the matter is that *The Kundalini Trilogy* is a massive shift in Consciousness Itself. What was communicated from master to disciple—a process that was only achieved because the disciple had the ability to recognise and articulate the experience—has now been set down in print. It is not a rule book or an invariant experience. It is like a map of the territory with the prominent landmarks and dangers clearly delineated. The terrain has to be traversed on your own, but now—and this is crucial—you know what is going on. This is incredible. So many times I would have unusual experiences that may have pushed one off balance, but I had seen the book, and it was comprehended instantly as just another stage of development. No need for fear nor for indulgence in anxiety, a message from Santosh that in the end may be the greatest value that *The Kundalini Trilogy* contributes to the world. All this fear mongering and expectation of huge sufferings if the kundalini activates is unwarranted. Santosh even calls the kundalini "the gentle force," and she is absolutely right. The process immediately calms down into manageable limits once you ask it to. It is astonishing to observe.

I am not going to run on about my guru, because no matter what I say in whatever flowery language, what I owe her and her books is a debt that cannot be repaid. In the end, there is only gratitude that the entire shakti latent in the book went to work on me first. After what happened with this supernatural trilogy, there is no doubt that Grace exists.

Shubhda Vaid

Coming from a traditional Marwari family background, I was a simple housewife busy with my routine life. On one of our holidays to a resort near Rishikesh and while taking part in a yoga session there, the visiting Australian teacher made us go through *yoga nidra*. My body started vibrating intensely. I felt as if I was above the ground, and I could see a profusion of light. After the session was over, I enquired about this experience from the teacher, but she dismissed it as just a stress release. After coming back to Mumbai, I continued with my yoga practice. While doing a session of focusing on chakras and reciting their *beej mantras* with my yoga instructor, I had the same experience again. When I narrated it to her, she told me to start meditating regularly to find out the meaning of my experience. I started looking around for answers, but a whirlpool of misconceptions, doubts, and misinformation was engulfing my total being and almost making me lose my mind.

While searching for answers, I came across a book called *Conscious Flight into the Empyrean* by Santosh Sachdeva, in which she mentioned some meditation classes at Churchgate in South Mumbai. I found her telephone number in the book, spoke with her, and she asked me to meet her. When we met, she enquired about what I was looking for. I was clueless. I told her I wanted to meet her guru and join his meditation classes. She told me that as he was not well, the classes were on hold for some time. In the hope of meeting him, I went to meet her again a couple of times, but every time her answer was the same as before. I do not know why I kept going to meet her. At our fourth meeting, she asked me, "You want to learn to meditate? Come. I will sit with you in meditation." I was thrilled and sat in front of her. She told me to look at a spot between her eyebrows and close my eyes after she closed her eyes. When I focused at the spot, I could see sharp rays of light emanating from her ajna chakra and entering mine. My eyes started burning, and my whole body went into a spin. I have no recollection of what happened next, but after the meditation, I knew that I had arrived at the right place. I came to know later that this was shaktipat and that what had happened at the yoga retreat was the *jagran* of kundalini shakti, which gave me unusual glimpses of light, vibration, and energy.

She asked me to start coming for her Thursday meditations. When I went for the first time, I realised that there was a group of elderly women there, of whom I was the youngest. Initially, it took me a few days to adjust to everyone's energy. While meditating, there were a few sounds that I had the involuntary urge to make, but I restrained this urge as I thought I would be disturbing the others. On sharing this with her, she told me to "relax and release" and not hold back anything. She asked me if I had old in-laws, parents, or children to look after. I replied in the affirmative. She advised me to be regular with my meditations, as this practice was not a game. Once on the path, I realised that the journey ahead was going to be not only nerve-racking but also adventurous and life changing. From that day, the intensity of my meditations increased manifold. There were times when I would growl, bark, hiss, cry, or laugh loudly. My body would go into an uncontrollable spin, or I would keep shaking my head vigorously. Other people at the group meditation were getting disturbed and upset over my behaviour. But Guruji (somewhere along the way, I had started calling her Guruji) explained to them about the kriyas that I was going through. In time, everyone became comfortable. With the process of sounds releasing from my body and with all the other kriyas that I was going through, the data of lifetimes was being released. During one of these meditations, I had this strong urge to touch her feet with my forehead, and that evening, throughout the meditation, I remained in this position, lying down at her feet. From that day onward, it became a ritual to touch Guruji's feet when meeting and leaving the group meditation.

As I started being in her energy field and her presence more and more, the shakti started unfolding many new experiences for me. Somewhere along the way, while continuing the meditations, I memorised the affirmations and started to recite them daily at home before meditation. Although I was not doing the breaths, the combined effect of regular meditation, reciting the affirmations, and being in her energy field soon started to result in different forms of experience. The words of the affirmations began coming alive for me and, through life situations and experiences, I started realising their true meaning. Limited thinking, strong conditionings, stifling relationships, fixed ideas—all started dropping off. Instead of being fixed and rigid in my views and opinions, I decided I would not force, and therefore stunt, my daughter's growth at the tender age of six with my own ambitions for her. I gave her enough space and provided the nurturing and loving atmosphere at home, which allowed her to develop her own beautiful personality.

I realised that trying to be always right and expecting others to always agree with me and forcing my opinions on them was the cause of marital disharmony at home. This understanding helped a lot in improving family relations. Somewhere along the way, the process of integration had finally started. From being judgmental and critical of everything, I started giving everyone a compassionate hearing. From coffees and conversations, the focus of my life soon shifted to satsangs and meditations. From wanting to be the centre of attention to wanting to be by myself even at a party, from trying to control each and every person and situation to allowing life to just flow—these changes started happening in all spheres of my life. These changes not only affected me but started affecting my near and dear ones in a positive way.

Everything was going fine till I went with my family for a holiday to the Maldives in 2011. Standing on a wooden plank in the vast ocean with no one to see for miles, I spread my hands up in the air to thank the Void for my guru, and I asked for the purpose of my life to be revealed. Little did I know what I had activated. The years to follow were cathartic. I felt like a rock on the shore of a rough sea with wave upon wave lashing me. The only thing that held me back from falling and being swept away was my guru's support and guidance. It was only the creative work that I started at her command and Grace, that helped me get over my insecurities and that turned me into an independent and confident woman. She made me realise my self-worth, giving me the power, courage, and stamina to face the world. I have now realised the true meaning of the word *transform*. I know this is not the end of growth. New challenges will keep coming, and I will keep meeting them with new understanding, faith, and confidence.

Rashmi Jokhakar

The most important phone call I ever made in my life was to Santosh "Aunty" (as I called her then) on December 11, 2013. My husband, Raman, and I had gotten to know about her about ten years ago, and we had both met her individually for a Tarot reading. We had come back, touched by her sweet, loving, and magnetic persona. When I was leaving after the reading, she casually mentioned that I could call her anytime if I ever had any questions. Over the years, I called her a few times, and eventually I met her. At one such meeting, she mentioned that I could come for group meditation at her place, which was held every Thursday. During those days, my daughter was still too small to leave her for very long. More to the point, I did not feel drawn to meditation, so I did not make an attempt to go.

Sometime around 2013, I started to feel an urge to meditate. One day, I was feeling gloomy and low. I remembered then that Santosh Aunty had told me about the meditations at her place. I called to ask her when she had the group meditation and whether I could come. It turned out there was a group meditation at seven that evening. I reached there on time and saw there were already a few people in the room. I sat on the floor, facing an empty chair. At five minutes to seven, she walked past me, placed her hand on my head, and said, "Oh! You are already here!" I smiled back at her. After taking her seat, she simply said, "I will look at your ajna chakra, and you look at mine. Then, we will start the meditation with the sound of Om. It will end thirty minutes later." After the meditation, she asked everyone to share their experience and then introduced me to the group. My memory of the first meditation with Guruji is as if it were only she and I in the room. Everyone and everything had simply vanished. Something inside me shifted; I felt much lighter and better. From that day onward, it was clear to me that I could never miss these meditations. As luck would have it, after I made that commitment to myself, nothing held me back.

It has been two and a half years now since I have been going for meditation at Guruji's place. Initially, during the meditations, I experienced a lot of movements—sometimes from side to side, sometimes forward and backward. Guruji always says that one should relax and let the energy do its work. Then there was a phase during which there would be strong jolts of energy shooting from the base of the spine all the way up to my head. It did not matter whether Guruji was physically there or not. The meditations always were, and are, equally potent.

I added the meditation practice to my morning routine of breathing exercises. Guruji told me that one should invoke the master each time one does any practice and seek blessings for one's practice. From her books, I learnt the importance of keeping to the same time and same place for my practice. Although I had been doing my breathing practice for many years, I had not paid attention to these basic essentials, which would make a world of difference.

I have noticed that my inner state transforms simply by spending some time in her presence. It does not matter what we are discussing. At times, just remembering her is enough. On one occasion, just before going to bed, I was emotional and teary about something. I remembered her and mentally bowed down to her. The next thing I knew, it was time to wake up, and I'd had the deepest and most restful sleep. For some reason, I have never felt the need to share this and other such experiences with her.

A certain transformation began from the day I started going for the meditations. I can now see that I was stuck in the mire of some self-defeating patterns, which would cause the same drama to repeat itself again and again and leave me in an abyss. Very soon, and without any conscious effort, I was freed from those clutches. It is no less than a miracle. When we share our experience after each meditation, it is like a snapshot, but each meditation sets in motion a deeper transformation. In due course, when one looks back, one understands how far one has reached. Personally, I think I have moved from being volatile to being much more stable. As I say this, I am reminded of the word *alchemy*. It is a work in progress.

Shyamala Mohan

With heartfelt joy and gratitude to my gurus, I would like to pen down thoughts about one very important turning point in my life.

I joined the basic Brahma Vidya Course on April 25, 2012. During the first lecture of the course, Guruji Suresh Mudaliar's words awakened the spiritual thirst lying deep within me. Guruji's conviction in his assurance, "I will show God inside you in the fourteenth week of our session," made me forget my body, mind, and intellect and directly touch the core of my inner being, which was on a search of many years for God. Another sentence of Guruji that had a deep impact on me was, "This course can be done by anybody, especially householders, by delivering all their daily chores with full attention." I experienced profound satisfaction that I had found what I was searching for.

In due course, I started to experience energy movements followed by kriyas. When I informed Guruji about this, his response was, "Don't pay much attention to what is happening. You are going to experience more as the practice goes on."

One day during meditation, I experienced very strong internal vibrations. Suddenly, I felt some energy dropping from my forehead and going down to the tip of my spine until it went back up. This was quite frightening and, at the same time, very exciting. I started thinking, "Is something wrong with me? Am I losing touch with my mundane life? What is happening to me? Should I stop or continue my sadhana?"

I realised that I was undergoing a spiritual experience and that, at this stage, right guidance from the right guru was necessary. I went to my guru and said, "I am experiencing vibrations internally. Will you guide me?" He asked me to join the advanced Brahma Vidya Course, the next level, for further guidance. He also told me that the experience must be a figment of my imagination. I felt deserted and needed someone to validate my experience. I started researching the Internet, trying to understand more about Brahma Vidya and its origins. I was searching for information about Guru Jyotirmayananda (Swami Ramanathan), the founder of the course in India, when I found a link that directed me to Santosh Ma's website. When I viewed her website, I felt that I had at last reached home. I was absorbing all that was described there. It came as a spring of nectar that I had been thirsting for. I understood that some of my experiences, of which I was not aware earlier, were the signs of kundalini awakening. I went through the details given on the website many times over. I then realised the importance of the right guru and the importance of the breaths that I had been practicing.

Then, I purchased Santosh Ma's books on kundalini. I would like to quote here the lines written on Santosh Ma's website about her guru:

> Guruji had certain questions for me. He wanted to know whether I had young children or old people to take care of. When I said no, he gave me the choice of continuing and contemplating on the process or stopping right there. He made me understand that once I got into the practice seriously, it would not be good to stop midway. I am very happy that I took up the challenge.

These lines made me think, "What will happen if I continue on this path? I am a householder with a grown-up child. My husband and son are very understanding, calm personalities." Then, I remembered my Guruji's words, "Brahma Vidya is for householders. By completing all your duties to your family, you can experience God." I had complete faith in his words. I believe the Divine Mother knows exactly what I need, so I will be guided well. After going through Santosh Ma's books, I was more confident and decided to continue on the path. It was so interesting and exciting; I felt like a child again and entered a fairyland. I started looking at everything within and without with a childlike curiosity.

The experiences written about in Santosh Ma's first book, *Conscious Flight into the Empyrean*, were so touching that I read it several times over. Sometimes, I would sit for a long time in bliss with wet eyes, thinking about the love and care God showers on us. I was living through the words written in that book. I was so excited, happy, and blissful…I can't express it in words. I truly found what I was looking for.

I felt deep devotion, gratitude, and reverence to the Divine Mother, who manifested to me through Amma (Mata Amritanandamayi Devi) and did all the ploughing in me for a seed to germinate. She was the one who directed me to Guruji and then to Santosh Ma in order for me to progress on my path and fulfil the purpose of my life. I felt a sense of great comfort.

I spoke openly about Santosh Ma and her work on the process of kundalini awakening with my fellow students of the advanced Brahma Vidya Course. Thereafter, they started concentrating more on their sadhana with a fearless mind. They also started having similar experiences as those described in her book. Then, thinking that we must inform Santosh Ma about the developments happening within us, we decided to meet Ma and express our gratitude to her for guiding us on this path. I wrote her a letter mentioning that four of us would like to meet her, as we were already using her book as a guide.

When we met on September 20, 2013, for the first time, we couldn't believe that we were meeting Ma personally. She was behaving so normal, just like any other human being. Instead of us expressing wonderment and awe, it was she who was expressing the same while hearing about our experiences. This was an amazing experience because I never imagined a realised soul would give so much love and importance to simple human beings like us, who were just beginners on the spiritual path. But she was seeing divinity in everything; the divine consciousness inside her was enjoying the excitement of other human beings on their journey. I could feel the oneness of the secret divine principle working through each person there in its unique way.

My yearning for the right guidance ended there, when I realised this truth. I had ultimately found my friend, guide, mentor, guru, God, mother. Everything in her matched my expectations of a spiritual master. After that, I started speaking to her regularly with full freedom, and I enjoyed her warmth and love. I would like to present here some of my letters to her and her replies to express how she guided me on my journey:

Dear Ma,

After talking to you yesterday, I was thinking and realised that you are always listening to me. I am telling you with excitement and joy that I am doing this and that, I am experiencing this and that, and so on. I have never asked you how you are or enquired about your well-being. So many things are getting more and more clear to me. When I am speaking to you, I feel like a chick who is taking warmth and care from a mother hen! How will I express this gratitude to you? I don't have any idea. The only thing I can do is to spread your message to more and more people and guide them toward you, whoever is on the path of evolution.

Sincerely,
Shyamala

Dear Shyamala,

I am grateful for your gratitude. It gives me a great sense of joy when I see a worthy aspirant move toward his/her goal to fulfil the purpose for which the experience is unfolding. It's also a wonder to see the role that is being fulfilled through this body, mind, intellect that is Santosh. Carry on, Shyamala. Go on joyfully and with a sense of wonder and a spirit of adventure of another kind.

Love,
Santosh Ma

Dear Ma,

It is still unbelievable for me that I am speaking to you, taking advice from you, and staying in touch with you.

It is still unbelievable for me that God answered my questions by guiding me toward you.

It is still unbelievable for me that I am realising so much inner meaning in everything that is happening in and around me day by day.

It is still unbelievable for me that the light (wisdom) is coming toward me and spreading back to the world day by day through my thoughts and actions.

It is still unbelievable for me that I am now unravelling the secret of my existence.

My understanding has gone far ahead since I joined Brahma Vidya. After meeting you, my speed is as if I were travelling by an airplane!

Please remove my ignorance. Protect me, guide me toward the ultimate goal of my existence!

I am grateful for all that ever was. I am grateful for all that there is. I am grateful for all that ever will be.

I question not the divine love, wisdom, and justice.

Happy Guru Pournima!
Forever in gratitude.
Shyamala

Love you, Shyamala. God bless.
Santosh Ma

Simple words, which touch my heart. I loved to share everything like a child shares her joy with her mother. The guiding is still continuing. Santosh Ma is love, light, happiness, and peace. She is healing me, emptying me, and recreating me by filling me up with divine love and happiness. I am grateful to my Guruji Suresh Mudaliar for imparting Brahma Vidya principles in their purest form and silently guiding me to Santosh Ma. Guruji is my spiritual father, and Santosh Ma is my spiritual mother. I am well protected and blessed!

Sanjay Vaid

I started practicing the Eight Spiritual Breaths about three years ago with blessings and guidance from Guruji Rohit Arya. At the very beginning, I was told by Guruji Rohit that the meditation is more powerful than the affirmations, and the affirmations are more powerful than the physical aspects of doing the breath itself. But somehow this was lost on me as I did not genuinely understand the implications. I did not in fact read the complete book on *The Eight Spiritual Breaths* by our prime Guruji Santosh Sachdeva except to refer to the affirmations and text related to the physical aspects of performing the breaths precisely. I did not even understand what the term *kundalini shakti* meant. Thus began my journey of living a "conscious life unconsciously," or doing things without being fully aware of their transformative implications.

The breaths gave me immense energy, enhanced my strength and immunity, and I never fell ill during the course of my practice. Perhaps this increased my arrogance, which got entangled with my prevalent anger and temperament, creating quite a mess. The energy, as I later learnt, enhances what is already prevalent as it is unable to distinguish between the good and bad.

Then about a year ago, within two years of starting my practice, I felt it was time for all other aspects of cleansing other than just the physical body. I got grounded. I had a series of experiences that were not life-threatening but were enough to give me a close, in-depth look at my way of life and the disturbance it caused in the universe. These experiences were, and are, very fortunate, and I am definitely blessed that I had close access to our prime Guruji, Santosh Sachdeva. I started spending as much time as I could to learn what was happening to me and henceforth live a conscious life—consciously.

I then realised that powerful affirmations do not only mean that I say them as loudly as I can but also that I believe and implement them in everyday life. I learnt to let go of the baggage I was carrying for all these years, as well as all the preconditioning, and see things with a new understanding and from the right perspective—to adhere to the everlasting, unchanging laws of the universe.

My journey has just begun, but I am confident and, in fact, certain of the joys that it would, and already has, started to unfold. Living with awareness and in harmony with the laws of the universe is what I look forward to practicing day after day. The joy I feel of being on this path—guided completely by the Eight Spiritual Breaths, as I strive for complete understanding from Guruji Santosh—is incomparable.

Radhika Chopra

When I met my guru, Santosh Ma, many years ago, I did not even consider having or needing a guru. I was looking for something to do, a few answers to my questions, and solutions to life's problems.

She was not a soothsayer, healer, or magician of any kind, so she was not the person I would bank on for my expectations to be fulfilled. Or so I thought.

I had started visiting her home for meditations once a week. I did not know what to expect, how to meditate, and what I would get out of it until one evening on a rainy day in July. Over a cup of tea with her, we spoke about the weather, children, the recent rainfall, and other mundane things of life.

During a particular moment of these discussions, something, a feeling, touched me. For a moment, I could not hear my thoughts nor her words. The feeling was overwhelming as it washed over me. I couldn't contain myself, and I burst into tears. I could see her face blurred through my tears. I felt something else, a Presence that pulled me. I could not understand it, and my mind struggled against the magnetic force that was enveloping me. That was the day I knew it. I did not know what it meant, but I knew it. I see her now as Shiva. Everything I thought I knew, everything I believed in, started to disintegrate. Like *Rudra roopa*, all chaos broke loose inside me, and a churning began that started to destroy the concepts and constructs of my mind. Such a deep silence prevailed in me at these times, and everything would simply fade away.

A thought would arise, and then the thought would dissolve. Within Shiva, all worlds are created and destroyed, and He alone is. She had only a few words to say, but I recognised that what she did not say in words was truly changing my world. Everything flowed in the space between two words.

I see her as Shakti. Her steps imprint every corner of my universe. She moves with unrelenting purpose, weeding out and breaking through all that is binding. Her love and gentle gaze soothes my soul like that of the Great Mother who has limitless compassion. My body comes alive. I feel the life force in my breath. I even hear her gentle whispers as I sit in her space.

For me, the whole is Her, the Ardhanarishwara, complete as One. What else can I seek, for I found the One.

Ramesh and Shoba Venugopal

The clairvoyance with which Santosh Ma has presented the information in *The Eight Spiritual Breaths* and the way the visualisations have come to her are so divine that many lifetimes of preparation must have gone into them. We extend to her our deep, heartfelt gratitude for the guidance.

We are evolving rapidly as a result of the course on the Eight Spiritual Breaths. Years of work have finally led us to the path of being able to actualise the experience of the Truth. It would be difficult to know where to start and where to end! We are constantly rereading the book chapter by chapter. Every time we read it, a new sentence pops up in our minds and reveals a deeper insight. This book is not written by a person but channelled with insight without involving the thinking mind.

It is just amazing how we are being made aware of our completeness through the course. Once during the practice, we automatically started chanting the "Shanti Padam" mantra from the Ishavasya Upanishad. The chant came up in our minds as if from some deep recesses of our memory.

What comes to mind is the work of David Bohm, the theoretical physicist, who coined the concepts of "implicate order" and "explicate order," which are enfolded within reality and which reveal themselves layer by layer when unfolded. As one begins to advance through the Eight Spiritual Breaths, each sentence unfolds like a lotus bud with infinite petals, yearning to reveal its multidimensional beauty upon every reading. Truth is revealed in this book depending upon the readiness of the *sadhak* to receive.

This is not simply a book. It is a life companion that you keep close to your heart and read every day until you and the book merge and become one. Blessed are those who get their hands on this book and Santosh Ma's teaching.

APPENDIX D

GLOSSARY

aarti Devotional prayer.

aasan Prayer rug.

achkan Knee-length overcoat.

agni-snan Literally, "the fire bath," a purification process practiced by tantrics.

ajna The sixth primary chakra in the body, according to Hindu tradition. It is a part of the brain that can be made more powerful through meditation, yoga, and other spiritual practices related to the point between the eyebrows.

alma mater The university, school, or college that one formerly attended.

anahata The fourth primary chakra in the heart region, according to Hindu Yoga, Shakta, and Buddhist Tantric traditions.

anekagra dhyan Multi-pointed focus.

Ardhanarishwara God as half man, half woman.

ashram Spiritual retreat, hermitage.

Atman Consciousness.

avasaram Opportunity.

baalis Earrings.

baraat Marriage procession.

Bebeji Paternal grandmother.

beej mantras A beej mantra is the shortest form of a mantra just like a beej (seed), which when sown grows into a tree. Similarly beej mantras of different gods, when recited together, give humans a lot of positive energy and the blessings of all the gods.

bhabhi Brother's wife.

bhaiya Brother.

Bhakti Path of devotion to achieve God-realisation.

bhandaras Preparation of food on large scale by devotees as a religious offering to a god. It is then distributed as prasad to all gathered devotees.

Brij Bhumi A region mainly in Uttar Pradesh around Mathura-Vrindavan. Brij, though never a clearly defined political region in India, is very well demarcated culturally. It is considered to be the land of Krishna.

chachi Father's sister.

chaddar Large decorative shawl or sheet of cloth, usually with some Islamic inscription, that is offered to be placed on the tomb of a Muslim pir, or revered sage. Muslim and Hindu women also use it as a head garment.

chakras Literally means "wheel" or "disc" in yogic literature. It is one of the several centres of consciousness located in the etheric body. A chakra is usually depicted as a lotus flower. Most texts on Kundalini Yoga agree upon seven main chakras: muladhara (in the region of the coccyx), which is the resting place of the dormant kundalini; svadhisthana (in the area of the generative organs), manipura (near the navel), anahata (in the heart region), vishuddhi (at the throat level), ajna (between the eyebrows), and the sahasrara, or the thousand-petalled lotus (at the top of the head). Each chakra is associated with a particular colour, sound, symbol, deity, planetary energy, and its own seed mantra.

chappal Sandals.

charanamrit Charged holy water.

chiku Sweet brown fruit of an evergreen tree grown widely in India.

chowkidar Caretaker.

dargah Tomb of a Muslim saint, a Muslim shrine.

darshan Ritual viewing to catch a glimpse of a divine personage.

deodar Variety of cedar growing in the Himalayas.

devi upasak Shakti path practitioner.

Devi yagna Fire sacrifice to the Goddess.

divya-drishti Intuitive perception achieved by yogis that enables them to see the past and future.

doshas Literally, "fault" or "disease."

Durga Fierce warrior-goddess regarded as the supreme power in the universe by some sects of Hinduism.

ekagra dhyan Single-pointed focus.

Ganpati Ganesha, the elephant-headed God of Knowledge, Arts, Wisdom, and Auspiciousness.

Gayatri mantra The supreme mantra. Also the presiding deity of the mantra, Gayatri is supposed to be the Mother of the Vedas.

gomatas Holy cows.

goonda Hired thug or bully.

goshala Cowshed.

hookah An oriental tobacco pipe with a long, flexible tube, which draws the smoke through water contained in a bowl.

ida One of the two main channels (lunar and left) within the body through which the kundalini ascends.

Ishavasya Upanishad One of the shortest treatises in the Upanishads. It discusses the Atman (Soul, Self) theory of Hinduism and is referenced by both Dvaita (dualism) and Advaita (non-dualism) schools of Vedanta.

jagran Awakening.

Janmashtami The birth anniversary of Lord Krishna, which usually falls sometime during August.

japa Chanting of the Divine name or mantra.

jiva Life; the individual self.

Jnana Yoga One of the main paths of yoga that a practitioner can follow on the path to Self-realisation. The word *jnana* comes from the Sanskrit term meaning "knowledge."

kahwah Traditional green tea preparation consumed in Kashmir Valley.

kamandalu Oblong water pot made of a dry gourd (pumpkin) or coconut shell, metal, wood of the Kamandalataru tree. Hindu ascetics or yogis often use it for carrying drinking water.

karmas Based on the principle of reincarnation, the system of divine justice whereby people face the results of their positive and negative thoughts and actions.

karmic Pertaining to karma and its unfolding.

Kashmiri Shaivism A school of the Tantric Shaiva tradition that originated in Kashmir between 700-1100 CE. Its followers believe in the all-powerful deity, Shiva, who symbolises universal, shared consciousness.

koshas Five sheaths that form the covering for the atman, or soul.

kriyas Breathing exercises and yoga postures.

kul guru Family guru.

Kundalini Yoga Branch of Yoga that is inner directed and is concerned primarily with the awakening of the kundalini and its consequent spiritual experiences.

kundalini The manifestation of the Dynamic Female Cosmic Energy within the individual body. Kundalini lies nascent in a coiled form at the base of the spine.

kurta-pyjama Typical Indian shirt and loose trousers.

lingam Symbol of Shiva.

Lord Shiva One of the Hindu Trinity, the androgynous god of destruction.

Lord Vishnu Literally, "He who pervades." One of the Hindu Trinity. Famed as the Protector and Rescuer.

Ma Tulja Bhavani An aspect of the Goddess.

Mahabharat Epic narrative of the Kurukshetra War between the Kaurava and the Pandava clans, in which Krishna, as the divine avatar of Vishnu, guided the Pandavas to victory..

mahants Senior sages.

Mahashakti The cosmic energy, or the dynamic female principle, symbolically depicted as the Great Goddess.

mala String of 108 sacred beads used in chanting for counting the exact number of mantra recitations. Doing one mala usually implies that a holy name or mantra is recited 108 times.

Mamaji Maternal uncle.

manas shakti Cosmic mind, mind power.

manipura The third primary chakra in the body, according to Hindu tradition. Associated with fire and the power of transformation (near the navel).

mantra diksha Formal spiritual initiation into a sacred lineage, usually with a special holy chant being assigned to the disciples according to their individual level of evolutionary growth.

mantras Sacred chants.

masi Mother's sister.

math Community temple.

maun vrat A vow of silence.

mudra A specific hand position in which the fingers are held for their symbolic or esoteric meaning. Each mudra conveys a certain message for the initiate, bringing an individual to a certain state of awareness.

muladhara The first primary chakra in the body, according to Hindu tradition. In the region of the coccyx, which is the resting place of the dormant kundalini (base chakra).

nadi Etheric channel for energy flow within the body. Out of a total of thirty-five million nadis in a human body, there are a hundred major ones. Among these, there are three main nadis: the pingala, or the solar nadi, on the right side of the spinal column; the ida, or the lunar nadi, located on the left side; and the sushumna, the most important one of all as the central nadi and the vehicle of balanced energy flow and spiritual growth.

Nataraja Shiva as the form of the Cosmic Dancer.

Nath Sampradaya A well-known religious sect, which has establishments all over India.

nimbu Lemon.

Om Shanti A mantra, greeting and parting salutation in Indian tradition. 'Om' is believed to be the sound of the universe, referred to as the cosmic vibration. 'Shanti' means 'peace.' One can say it means 'Peace be unto you.'

Padma Shri One of the highest civilian honours of India.

Padma Vibhushan Second-highest civilian award of India.

pandit Scholar or a teacher of any field of knowledge in Hinduism, particularly the Vedic scriptures, dharma, and Hindu philosophy.

A pandit might also teach secular subjects, such as music. He may be a guru in a gurukul.

Paramatman Cosmic Consciousness. In Hindu theology, Paramatman is the "Absolute Atman," or "Supreme Soul," in the Vedanta and Yoga philosophies of India.

parampara Tradition.

Pavan Putra Hanuman Another name for Hanuman, which means "son of Vayu, the wind god."

pedas Sweet made with milk.

pehlwaan Wrestler.

pingala One of the two main channels (solar and right) within the body through which the kundalini ascends.

Praji Elder brother.

prana Life Force or vital energy, which constitutes the breath in living beings.

pranaams Reverential form of greeting.

pranamaya kosha The collection of five vital energies, namely prana, apana, udana, vyana, and samana. In the physical body, it refers to that level of life force that provides movement and activity to the physical body and the sense organs.

prasad Consecrated offerings infused with sacred energy and returned for consumption by the devotees.

puja The formal mode of conducting prayers, whether in private or in public.

Puranas Compilations of Hindu mythic tales of the gods and goddesses.

Ram mantra Chanting of Lord Ram's name, such as the Sanskrit chant, *Sri Ram, Jai Ram, Jai Jai Ram.*

rishis Sages who have realised Brahman. There are distinctions of expertise amongst rishis.

Rudra roopa Rudra is a former manifestation of Lord Shiva mentioned in the Rigveda, where he has been praised as the 'mightiest of the mighty.'

saat patti Card game played with seven cards.

sadhak Aspirant on the spiritual path who undertakes ascetic practices.

sadhana Adoption of meditation, asceticism, and devotional practices on the spiritual path.

sadhus Holy men, renunciants, wandering mendicants on a pilgrimage.

sahasrara Crown centre, the seventh primary chakra, which, according to most tantric yoga traditions, is at the top of the head.

salwar-kurta A traditional outfit originating in the Indian subcontinent.

samadhi One of the final stages of meditation, when the aspirant enters what appears to be a trance state and experiences an absence of a body or ego consciousness. The experience in meditation of Oneness and Cosmic Unity.

sannyasins Female sannyasis, renunciants on the spiritual path.

sannyasis Renunciants on the spiritual path.

sardar Respectful term of address for Sikh males. They are identified by their distinctive turbans and beards.

sari Garment of cotton or silk elaborately draped around the body, traditionally worn by women from South Asia.

satsang Being with good and righteous companions in the company of a sage.

sehra A floral veil.

shaktipat Energy transmission from the guru or a Higher Source to the disciple, bringing about an evolutionary transformation of consciousness.

shastras Sciences, Hindu scriptures.

shishya Student, disciple.

Shiva lingam The symbolic form by which Shiva is worshipped.

Shiva mantra *Om Namah Shivaya.* The basic mantra chanted by the devotees of Lord Shiva.

siddhis Powers that arise within the person with the rigorous practice of yoga. Clairvoyance and levitation are two examples.

Sikh A follower of Sikhism—a religion that developed around 15-16 CE and separated from Hinduism. It is based on the belief in a single god, and on the teachings of Guru Nanak.

sitar Stringed musical instrument.

sushumna The nadi, or energy channel, that leads to the sacral chakra.

swami A God-realised person of one of the several monastic orders, who practices renunciation, celibacy, and asceticism and who hence represents spiritual authority.

swastik A religious symbol for Hindus, the swastik signifies many things—Surya (the sun), and Brahma, the creator. It is also seen as a power symbol and is the emblem of Ganesha, the god of good luck.

tantric One who practices tantra, one of the yogic disciplines.

tava A large, flat, disc-shaped frying pan.

tilak A mark applied on the forehead to signify one's sectarian status.

tonga Buggy, an old form of horse-drawn carriage.

topi cap

toran A decorative floral or fabric door hanging, put up on the occasion of festivals or weddings.

totkas Charms and spells.

trishul Trident, a weapon associated with Shiva.

uthala According to Hindu tradition, this rite usually takes place on the fourth day after the funeral rites have been performed.

vaak siddhi Mastery gained to make predictions that come true.

vairagya Renunciation of desire and attachment to material forms.

veena Indian multi-stringed musical instrument.

vibhuti Ash from a sacred fire.

vishuddhi The fifth primary chakra in the body, according to Hindu tradition. Vishuddhi is positioned at the throat region near the spine.

yagna Fire sacrifice of the Hindus.

yantra An abstract geometric pattern that signifies the unique characteristics of a deity or group of deities.

yin-yang Chinese symbol representing the male and female cosmic energy.

yoga nidra Yogic practice that induces the deepest possible states of relaxation while still maintaining full consciousness.

Yoga Union of the individual consciousness with the Absolute through the systematic practice of meditation, based on the eightfold path prescribed by the ancient sage Patanjali.

For information on Santosh Sachdeva, visit:
www.santoshsachdeva.com

The author may be contacted on email:
mails@santoshsachdeva.com

For further details, contact:
Yogi Impressions LLP
1711, Centre 1, World Trade Centre,
Cuffe Parade, Mumbai 400 005, India.

Fill in the Mailing List form on our website
and receive, via email, information on
books, authors, events and more.
Visit: www.yogiimpressions.com

Telephone: (022) 61541500, 61541541
E-mail: yogi@yogiimpressions.com

ALSO PUBLISHED BY YOGI IMPRESSIONS

Hindi

Marathi

The Eight Spiritual Breaths:

Breathing Exercises and Affirmations That Transform Your Life

by Santosh Sachdeva

After migrating to Tibet, the renowned yogi and teacher Padmasambhava of Nalanda University developed a set of breathing exercises to help human beings actualise their highest potential. Eventually this course came to India and was taught in Mumbai, where the author completed it under the guidance of a spiritual teacher. In *The Eight Spiritual Breaths*, she brings a modern perspective to these breathing exercises and shows how they can help spiritual aspirants to gain mastery across all dimensions in their lives.

The Eight Spiritual Breaths can help you to

- Improve memory retention
- Increase states of calmness
- Attain your personal goals
- Enhance creative potential
- Revitalise health and energy levels